The Smoothies Bible

Publications International, Ltd.

Pictured on the front cover *(top to bottom):* Fruity Smoothie *(page 96)* and Strawberry Mango Smoothie *(page 50).*

Pictured on the back cover *(top to bottom):* Going Green *(page 52),* Carrot Cake Smoothie *(page 112)* and Strawberry Sundae Smoothie *(page 126).*

ISBN-13: 978-1-4508-5849-6
ISBN-10: 1-4508-5849-X

Library of Congress Control Number: 2012941405

Manufactured in China.

8 7 6 5 4 3 2 1

Nutritional Analysis: Every effort has been made to check the accuracy of the nutritional information that appears with each recipe. However, because numerous variables account for a wide range of values for certain foods, nutritive analyses in this book should be considered approximate. Different results may be obtained by using different nutrient databases and different brand-name products.

Microwave Cooking: Microwave ovens vary in wattage. Use the cooking times as guidelines and check for doneness before adding more time.

Preparation/Cooking Times: Preparation times are based on the approximate amount of time required to assemble the recipe before cooking, baking, chilling or serving. These times include preparation steps such as measuring, chopping and mixing. The fact that some preparations and cooking can be done simultaneously is taken into account. Preparation of optional ingredients and serving suggestions is not included.

Publications International, Ltd.

Table of Contents

Introduction.. 4

Breakfast *Blends*.................................... 8

Fruit-Packed *Favorites*.........................34

Just for *Kids*..58

Healthy *Sips* 84

Drinkable *Desserts* 108

Shake It *Up*..134

Summer *Drinks*....................................158

Acknowledgments...................................184

Index..185

Thick, delicious, refreshing smoothies—they're easy to prepare, delightful to drink, budget friendly and perfect for all ages. Preparing smoothies at home not only saves money, but also spares you the added sugar and juice most restaurants use.

A blender and a handful of ingredients are the basic necessities for preparing the recipes in this cookbook. When using fresh fruits and vegetables, choose ones that are ripe, free from blemishes and have a pleasant aroma. Have your glasses ready before starting a recipe, so you can serve the smoothies immediately after preparation.

Blenders

Blenders are the most common equipment used to make smoothies. They are excellent for mixing drinks, puréeing food and making smooth sauces. There are two types of blenders: countertop and hand-held/immersion blenders. They come in a variety of colors, speeds and controls. The key to the perfect smoothie blender is having enough power to crush ice. Each blender has its own advantages, so choose the one that is best suited to your needs.

Countertop blenders sit on a countertop or tabletop during operation. The removable blender container can be made of glass, plastic or stainless steel and holds from 5 to 8 cups. Inside the blender container, there are blades that turn at different speeds to blend the ingredients to their desired consistency. Some basic blenders have 3 speeds; more advanced models may have up to 16 speeds.

Hand-held/immersion blenders are portable and convenient—there is no removable container; the mixing head with rotating blades is submerged into saucepans, bowls or glasses. There are usually only 3 speeds on this type of blender.

Ingredients

Fresh fruits and vegetables make the best-tasting smoothies. But if you need to use produce that is not in season, you may substitute frozen. The basic rule of thumb when choosing fresh fruits or vegetables is to make sure they are ripe, free from blemishes and have a pleasant aroma.

The fruits listed below are used commonly throughout this cookbook. Additional tips on selection, ripening and/or storing are provided.

Bananas: Bananas are picked and shipped green. By the time they reach the supermarket, they are almost ripe. Choose bananas that are plump and have not yet become fully yellow, so they will be firm and free of bruises when you get them home. To ripen bananas, simply store at room temperature. To speed ripening, place them in an unsealed paper bag.

Berries: Look for berries that are firm, plump, and fresh looking. If the berries are packed in a clear plastic container, turn the container over and check for moldy or crushed berries. If they are packed in a paperboard container, look for juice stains on the bottom of the container—this indicates crushed berries and possible mold.

Cherries: Choose plump, firm fruits with glossy skin and no bruises or leakage. Cherries don't ripen after picking, so immature cherries (marked by small size and poor color) should be avoided. Cherries with stems attached keep longer.

Coconuts: The hairy shell of the coconuts sold in supermarkets is actually the second layer that is marked by three indentations or "eyes." There should be no leakage from any of the eyes. The coconut should be heavy for its size and brown, not grey in color.

Kiwi: This fuzzy brown-skinned fruit has a succulent, emerald green flesh that will yield to gentle pressure when ripe, but usually needs additional ripening after purchase. Choose fruit without mold or soft spots.

Lemons: Lemons should be firm and heavy for their size, with no sign of green. Thin-skinned lemons usually yield more juice. To get the most juice, warm lemons to room temperature and press down with the palm of your hand as you roll them on the countertop before squeezing.

Limes: Select firm, heavy fruit that has a natural sheen to its skin. Avoid limes that appear to be dried out or that are light for their size.

Small brown patches on the skin, called scald, are not an indication of poor quality. To get the most juice, use the same technique as with lemons.

Mangoes: Mangoes should be firm but not hard—rock-hard mangoes most likely will rot before they ripen. The skin should be taut, smooth and free of black spots and shriveled ends. A sweet, fruity aroma around the stem end is indicative of a good selection.

Oranges: Select heavy, firm fruits with no signs of mold on the skin or softening at the blossom end. The skin should have a natural luster. Avoid those that look dull.

Peaches: Peaches should have a soft, downy covering of white fuzz and be streaked with both pink and yellow. There are two varieties of peaches—white and yellow. To ripen, store peaches at room temperature or place in a loosely closed paper bag or fruit-ripening bowl until they yield to gentle palm pressure.

Pineapples: Select a pineapple that is heavy for its size and has crown leaves that are dark green and fresh looking. A green color is not an indication that the fruit is unripe, so be sure to use the smell test rather than the color test.

Pomegranates: This spherical fruit has bright coral-red, leathery skin and an abundance of juicy garnet-colored seeds which have a tantalizing, sweet-and-sour taste. Juice can be extracted from a pomegranate half with a citrus juicer or purchased in the supermarket.

Watermelons: A ripe watermelon will have a shrunken, discolored stem and will produce a hollow sound when thumped with your knuckles. The end nearest the stem is usually the sweetest. The flesh may be red, yellow, orange or pink.

Serving and Garnishing

Smoothies should be served immediately after preparing them for the best flavor and texture, so you will need to have all the glassware and garnishes ready before you begin the recipe. Look at the photography in this cookbook to give you additional ideas for glassware, colored straws, stirrers and garnishes. The simple ideas below are just a few of the many ways to garnish a smoothie.

Recipe Ingredients

For a simple garnish, choose an ingredient like a strawberry, lemon, lime or an herb from the ingredient list. Place it on the rim of the glass or float it on top of the smoothie. Small pieces of fruit on toothpicks also make nice garnishments.

Fruit and Chocolate Curls

A vegetable peeler may be used to easily create fruit and chocolate curls. When making a fruit curl, be careful to remove only the colored part of the peel with the vegetable peeler, not the bitter white pith. The peel may then be cut into thinner strips, if desired. Twist the strips around straws and then place the straws in ice water in the refrigerator to set the curl.

For chocolate curls, place one 1-ounce square of semisweet chocolate per serving on a microwavable plate and microwave on HIGH 5 to 10 seconds. (Chocolate should still be firm.) Pull the vegetable peeler across the chocolate to create curls. Place them on a waxed paper-lined baking sheet and refrigerate 15 minutes or until firm.

Glassware Rims

Glassware rims can be coated with sugar, coconut or even graham cracker crumbs. To create extra-fine coatings, place them in the blender and pulse until the desired texture is reached. It is easiest to place the coatings in small bowls that fit the entire rim of the glass. Wet the rims with water or fruit juice, then dip in the desired coatings.

Breakfast Blends

Energy Smoothie

1 package (16 ounces) frozen unsweetened strawberries, partially thawed

2 medium ripe bananas

1 cup vanilla soymilk or milk*

1 container (6 ounces) lemon or vanilla yogurt

⅓ cup powdered sugar

2 teaspoons vanilla

*If using milk, add 1 to 2 tablespoons additional sugar, if desired.

1. Combine strawberries, bananas, soymilk, yogurt, powdered sugar and vanilla in blender; blend until smooth.

2. Pour into four glasses. Serve immediately.   *Makes 4 servings*

Tip: If all of the ingredients will not fit into the blender, blend all ingredients except 1 banana until smooth. Add remaining banana and blend until smooth.

Jump Start Smoothie

2 cups V8 SPLASH® Mango Peach Juice Drink, chilled

1 cup low-fat vanilla yogurt

2 cups frozen whole strawberries or raspberries

Put all the ingredients in a blender. Cover and blend until smooth. Serve immediately. *Makes 4 servings*

Prep Time: 5 minutes
Total Time: 5 minutes

Banana Smoothie

**1 packet CREAM OF WHEAT® Maple Brown Sugar
Instant Hot Cereal, uncooked**

⅔ cup boiling water

1 large banana

1 cup ice cubes

**1 teaspoon MAPLE GROVE FARMS® of Vermont
Pure Maple Syrup or honey**

Place Cream of Wheat and boiling water in blender container; cover. Blend on low speed 1 minute. Add banana; blend 30 seconds longer. Add ice and maple syrup; cover. Blend on high speed until smooth. Serve immediately. *Makes 2 servings*

Tip: Use CREAM OF WHEAT® Apples 'n Cinnamon, Strawberries 'n Cream or Cinnamon Swirl Instant Hot Cereal to create new delicious flavors.

Prep Time: 5 minutes
Total Time: 10 minutes

Jump Start Smoothies

Berry-Banana Breakfast Smoothie

1 container (6 ounces) berry yogurt

1 ripe banana, cut into chunks

½ cup milk

1. Combine yogurt, banana and milk in blender; blend until smooth.

2. Pour into two glasses. Serve immediately.   *Makes 2 servings*

Chai Soy Protein Smoothie

⅓ cup ALLWHITES®

4 ounces refrigerated soy milk, warmed*

2 tablespoons dry instant chai latte mix**

1 container (6 ounces) soy vanilla or peach yogurt

½ cup ice

*Soy milk and soy yogurt can be found in the refrigerated health or natural food section of your grocery store.
**Instant chai latte mix can be found in the instant coffee section of your grocery store.

Stir together warm soy milk and latte mix in glass until mix is dissolved. Combine chai, milk, ALLWHITES® and yogurt in blender. Cover and blend on medium speed until smooth. Add ice; blend until smooth. Serve immediately.   *Makes 1 (16-ounce) serving*

Prep Time: 5 minutes

Berry-Banana Breakfast Smoothies

Irish Cream Iced Cappuccino

1 cup water
½ cup cocoa
½ cup instant coffee granules
½ cup EQUAL® SPOONFUL*
6 cups fat-free milk
½ cup liquid Irish cream coffee creamer

*May substitute 12 packets EQUAL® sweetener.

- Whisk together first 3 ingredients in large saucepan until smooth. Bring to a boil over medium heat, whisking constantly. Boil 2 minutes, whisking constantly. Remove mixture from heat; stir in Equal®. Cool slightly.

- Whisk in milk and creamer. Cover and chill at least 4 hours or up to 2 days.

- Serve over ice.   *Makes 8 servings*

Apple Smoothie

3 cups Michigan Apple cider or Michigan Apple juice
1 cup vanilla lowfat yogurt
1 package (3.4 ounces) instant vanilla pudding mix
Apple pie spice (optional)

In small bowl, combine Michigan Apple cider, yogurt and pudding mix. Whisk with wire whip until smooth. Refrigerate 2 hours before serving. Sprinkle with apple pie spice just before serving, if desired.

Makes 4 servings

*Favorite recipe from **Michigan Apple Committee***

Irish Cream Iced Cappuccinos

Blueberry Banana Oatmeal Smoothie

½ cup frozen blueberries

1 banana

1 cup milk

½ cup plain yogurt

¼ cup uncooked quick oats

Fresh mint (optional)

1. Combine blueberries, banana and milk in blender; blend until smooth. Add yogurt and oats; blend 10 to 15 seconds or until well combined.

2. Pour into two glasses. Garnish with mint. Serve immediately.

Makes 2 servings

Glorious Morning Smoothie

1 cup frozen strawberries

1 cup Fat Free French Vanilla STONYFIELD FARM® Yogurt

1 cup orange juice

3 tablespoons wheat germ

Place ingredients into blender and mix on high until smooth. Garnish with a fresh strawberry.

Makes 2 tall smoothies

Blueberry Banana Oatmeal Smoothies

Morning Glory Cream Fizz

- 1 banana, cut into chunks
- 1 cup cubed papaya or mango
- 1 container (6 ounces) vanilla yogurt
- 3 tablespoons half-and-half or milk
- 1 tablespoon honey
- ½ cup club soda or sparkling water, chilled
- Ground nutmeg and papaya slices (optional)

1. Combine banana, papaya cubes, yogurt, half-and-half and honey in blender; blend until nearly smooth. Gently stir in club soda.

2. Pour into three glasses. Sprinkle with nutmeg and garnish with papaya slices. Serve immediately. *Makes 3 servings*

Wake-Me-Up Breakfast Smoothie

- 2 cups sliced strawberries
- 2 containers (6 ounces each) vanilla yogurt
- 1½ cups ice cubes
- 1 banana
- ½ cup milk
- 2 tablespoons wheat germ
- 1 tablespoon maple syrup

1. Combine strawberries, yogurt, ice, banana, milk, wheat germ and maple syrup in blender; blend until smooth.

2. Pour into six glasses. Serve immediately. *Makes 6 servings*

Morning Glory Cream Fizz

Spiced Maple, Banana & Oatmeal Smoothie

½ cup ice cubes

1 frozen banana

¼ cup milk

½ cup yogurt

¼ cup uncooked quick oats

1 tablespoon maple syrup, plus additional for garnish

Dash ground cinnamon

Dash ground nutmeg

Whipped cream and cinnamon stick (optional)

1. Place ice in blender; blend to crush. Add banana and milk; blend until smooth. Add yogurt, oats, 1 tablespoon maple syrup, cinnamon and nutmeg; blend until smooth.

2. Pour into two glasses. Garnish with whipped cream and cinnamon stick. Drizzle with additional maple syrup. Serve immediately.

Makes 2 servings

Frozen fruit will make a smoothie colder without diluting the flavor with additional ice.

Spiced Maple, Banana & Oatmeal Smoothie

Berry Morning Medley

1½ **cups milk**

1 **cup frozen mixed berries**

½ **cup plain yogurt**

1 **tablespoon sugar**

¼ **teaspoon vanilla**

¼ **cup granola, plus additional for garnish**

1. Combine milk and berries in blender; blend until mixture is thick and creamy. Add yogurt, sugar and vanilla; blend until smooth. Add ¼ cup granola; pulse 15 to 20 seconds.

2. Pour into two glasses. Sprinkle with additional granola. Serve immediately. *Makes 2 servings*

Guava Smoothie

1½ **cups (11.5 fluid-ounce can) guava nectar, chilled**

⅔ **cup (5 fluid-ounce can) NESTLÉ® CARNATION® Evaporated Milk,** *chilled*

½ **cup ice cubes**

2 **tablespoons granulated sugar**

PLACE nectar, evaporated milk, ice and sugar in blender; cover. Blend until smooth. *Makes 2 servings*

Variations: Other nectar flavors such as strawberry banana, mango, pineapple coconut or papaya can be substituted for the guava.

Prep Time: 5 minutes

Berry Morning Medley

Banana-Pineapple Breakfast Shake

2 cups plain yogurt

1 cup ice cubes

1 can (8 ounces) crushed pineapple in juice, undrained

1 medium ripe banana

5 to 6 tablespoons sugar

1 teaspoon vanilla

⅛ teaspoon ground nutmeg

1. Combine yogurt, ice, pineapple, banana, sugar, vanilla and nutmeg in blender; blend until smooth.

2. Pour into four glasses. Serve immediately.   *Makes 4 servings*

Blueberry Pomegranate Fruit Smoothie

1 cup boiling water

4 LIPTON® Blueberry & Pomegranate Flavor Pyramid Tea Bags

2 tablespoons sugar

1 cup frozen strawberries

1 pint (2 cups) frozen nonfat vanilla yogurt

Pour boiling water over LIPTON® Blueberry & Pomegranate Flavor Pyramid Tea Bags; cover and brew 5 minutes. Remove Tea Bags and squeeze. Stir in sugar until dissolved; chill.

In blender, process tea mixture with remaining ingredients until smooth. Serve immediately.   *Makes 4 servings*

Prep Time: 10 minutes
Brew Time: 5 minutes
Chill Time: 1 hour

Banana-Pineapple Breakfast Shakes

Breakfast Mocha Java

    3 cups milk

    3 eggs

    5 to 6 tablespoons sugar

    3 tablespoons unsweetened cocoa powder

    2 teaspoons instant coffee granules

1½ teaspoons vanilla

1. Combine milk, eggs, sugar, cocoa, coffee and vanilla in blender; blend until smooth.

2. Pour into four glasses. Serve immediately. *Makes 4 servings*

Serving Suggestion: This rich and delicious shake also tastes great served over ice.

Cherry Smoothie

    2 cups frozen tart cherries

    1 ripe banana, peeled

    1 cup 100% ready-to-drink tart cherry juice

    Maraschino cherries and pineapple chunks (optional)

Put frozen cherries, banana and cherry juice in container of electric blender or food processor. Purée until smooth. Pour into individual serving glasses. Garnish with maraschino cherries and pineapple, if desired. Serve immediately. *Makes 4 servings*

*Favorite recipe from **Cherry Marketing Institute***

Breakfast Mocha Javas

Breakfast Pom Smoothie

1 small ripe banana
½ cup mixed berries, plus additional for garnish
¾ cup pomegranate juice
⅓ to ½ cup soymilk or milk

1. Combine banana and ½ cup berries in blender; blend until smooth. Add juice and soymilk; blend until smooth.

2. Pour into glass. Garnish with additional berries. Serve immediately.

Makes 1 serving

Variations: You can substitute any pomegranate juice blend for the pomegranate juice. You can also substitute yogurt for the soymilk.

DOLE® Sunrise Smoothie

1 cup DOLE® Pineapple Juice
1 cup vanilla low-fat yogurt or frozen yogurt
1 cup DOLE® Frozen Sliced or Whole Strawberries, partially thawed
2 ripe, medium DOLE® Bananas, peeled

• Combine pineapple juice, yogurt, strawberries and bananas in blender or food processor container. Cover; blend until smooth. Garnish with strawberries and banana slices, if desired. *Makes 4 servings*

Prep Time: 10 minutes

Breakfast Pom Smoothie

Vermont Maple Smoothie

3 containers (½ cup each) unsweetened applesauce *or*
   1½ cups unsweetened applesauce

1 cup vanilla frozen yogurt

1 cup milk

2 ice cubes

3 tablespoons maple syrup

½ teaspoon ground cinnamon

  Ground nutmeg (optional)

1. Combine applesauce, yogurt, milk, ice, maple syrup and cinnamon in blender; blend until smooth.

2. Pour into four glasses. Sprinkle with nutmeg. Serve immediately.

Makes 4 servings

Sunrise Smoothie

8 ounces frozen unsweetened peach slices, partially thawed

8 ounces vanilla yogurt

1 cup ice cubes

1 can (6 ounces) pineapple juice

3 to 4 tablespoons sugar

1 tablespoon lemon juice

¼ to ½ teaspoon almond extract

1. Combine peaches, yogurt, ice, pineapple juice, sugar, lemon juice and almond extract in blender; blend until smooth.

2. Pour into two glasses. Serve immediately.   *Makes 2 servings*

Vermont Maple Smoothies

Rise 'n' Shine Smoothie

½ cup uncooked oats

1 cup orange juice

6 ounces vanilla yogurt

½ cup vanilla soymilk

4 strawberries

3 ice cubes

1 teaspoon cinnamon (optional)

1. Place oats in blender; blend into fine crumbs. Add orange juice, yogurt, soymilk, strawberries and ice; blend until well combined.

2. Pour into two glasses. Sprinkle with cinnamon. Serve immediately.

Makes 2 servings

Tropical Sunrise

1 frozen banana

1 cup frozen mango chunks

1 cup pineapple chunks

⅓ cup light coconut milk

⅓ cup orange juice

1¾ cups plain yogurt

1. Combine banana, mango, pineapple, coconut milk and orange juice in blender; blend until smooth. Add yogurt; blend until smooth.

2. Pour into glasses. Serve immediately.

Makes 2 to 4 servings

Rise 'n' Shine Smoothie

Fruit-Packed Favorites

Blueberry Pomegranate Smoothie with Honey & Orange

1 can (12 fluid ounces) NESTLÉ® CARNATION® Evaporated
    Fat Free Milk*

2 cups frozen blueberries

1 cup pomegranate juice**

¼ cup frozen orange juice concentrate

2 tablespoons honey or more to taste

½ cup ice cubes

*Substitute CARNATION® Evaporated Lowfat 2% Milk for fat free milk.
**Substitute cranberry juice for pomegranate juice.

PLACE evaporated milk, blueberries, juice, concentrate, honey and ice in blender; cover. Blend until smooth. Pour into tall glasses and serve immediately.
Makes 4 servings

Prep Time: 5 minutes

Mango-Ginger Smoothie

2 cups cubed mango

2½ cups peaches, peeled and sliced

1 cup ice cubes

1 container (6 ounces) vanilla yogurt

2 tablespoons honey

2 teaspoons grated fresh ginger

Mango and candied ginger slices (optional)

1. Combine 2 cups mango, peaches, ice, yogurt, honey and grated ginger in blender; blend until smooth.

2. Pour into four glasses. Garnish with mango and ginger slices. Serve immediately. *Makes 4 servings*

Grape Roughie

½ cup Chilean seedless green grapes

½ cup 1% milk

½ cup plain low-fat yogurt

1 tablespoon brown sugar

⅛ teaspoon vanilla

2 ice cubes

Place all ingredients in blender. Blend at high speed 15 seconds or until smooth. Serve immediately. *Makes 1 serving*

*Favorite recipe from **Chilean Fresh Fruit Association***

Mango-Ginger Smoothies

Blueberry Pineapple Smoothie

2 cups fresh or frozen blueberries, plus additional for garnish
1½ cups diced pineapple
1 cup pineapple juice
1 to 3 ice cubes
Pineapple chunks (optional)

1. Combine 2 cups blueberries, pineapple and pineapple juice in blender; blend until smooth. Add 3 ice cubes if using fresh fruit or 1 to 2 ice cubes if using frozen fruit; blend until smooth.

2. Pour into two glasses. Garnish with additional blueberries and pineapple chunks. Serve immediately. *Makes 2 servings*

Fruity Green Tea Smoothie

1 cup boiling water
4 LIPTON® Green Tea Bags, any variety
2 tablespoons sugar
½ medium ripe banana
½ cup ice cubes (about 3 to 4)

In teapot, pour boiling water over LIPTON® Green Tea Bags; cover and brew 1½ minutes. Remove Tea Bags. Stir in sugar and chill.

In blender, process tea, banana and ice cubes until blended. Garnish, if desired, with orange wheels. *Makes 2 servings*

Blueberry Pineapple Smoothie

Raspberry Peach Perfection Smoothie

1½ cups fresh or frozen peach slices, plus additional for garnish
1 cup peach nectar
1 container (6 ounces) raspberry yogurt
¾ cup fresh or frozen raspberries, plus additional for garnish
1 tablespoon honey (optional)
1 to 3 ice cubes

1. Combine 1½ cups peaches, nectar, yogurt, ¾ cup raspberries and honey, if desired, in blender; blend until smooth. Add 3 ice cubes if using fresh fruit and 1 to 2 ice cubes if using frozen fruit; blend until smooth.

2. Pour into two glasses. Garnish with additional peaches and raspberries. Serve immediately. *Makes 2 servings*

Watermelon Kiwi Smoothie

2 cups seedless watermelon chunks
2 kiwis, peeled and chopped
2 cups vanilla yogurt
1 cup ice
2 sprigs fresh mint

Place watermelon, kiwis, yogurt and ice in blender and purée until smooth. Pour into 2 glasses and garnish each with mint sprig.

Makes 2 servings

*Favorite recipe from **National Watermelon Promotion Board***

Raspberry Peach Perfection Smoothies

Island Delight Smoothie

> **2 cups chopped mango**
> **1 container (16 ounces) plain yogurt**
> **1½ cups ice cubes**
> **1½ cups pineapple-orange juice, chilled**
> **1 cup chopped pineapple**
> **1 frozen banana**
> **½ cup sliced strawberries**
> **2 tablespoons honey**
>   **Fresh banana slices (optional)**

1. Combine mango, yogurt, ice, pineapple-orange juice, pineapple, frozen banana, strawberries and honey in blender; blend until smooth.

2. Pour into four glasses. Garnish with banana slices. Serve immediately.

Makes 4 servings

Tip

To prepare a mango, hold it stem end up. Make vertical cuts on the two flat sides of the mango from the top to the bottom about ½ inch to the right of the stem. Score the flesh with the tip of the knife. Gently push the skin side toward you so the flesh separates. Run a table knife between the skin and the flesh to separate the cubes. Peel the sections still attached to the mango and slice the flesh from the seed.

Island Delight Smoothies

Cranberry Orange Smoothie

        2 cups fresh or frozen peach slices
    1¼ cups orange juice
      ½ cup whole berry cranberry sauce
      1 to 3 ice cubes
        Fresh orange slices and cranberries (optional)

1. Combine peaches, orange juice and cranberry sauce in blender; blend until smooth. Add 3 ice cubes if using fresh fruit or 1 to 2 ice cubes if using frozen fruit; blend until smooth.

2. Pour into two glasses. Garnish with orange slices and cranberries. Serve immediately.   *Makes 2 servings*

Nectarine Cantaloupe Smoothie

        1 fresh California nectarine, halved, pitted and cubed
        1 cup cubed cantaloupe
      ½ cup plain low-fat yogurt
        1 teaspoon honey
        3 ice cubes

Add nectarine and cantaloupe to food processor or blender. Process until smooth. Stir in yogurt, honey and ice just until blended. Serve immediately.   *Makes 2 servings*

*Favorite recipe from **California Tree Fruit Agreement***

Cranberry Orange Smoothies

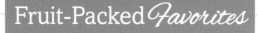
Cranberry Pineapple Smoothie

2 cups Cranberry Pineapple Smoothie Base (recipe follows)
1 large ripe banana (optional)
4 cups ice cubes
  Orange peel and mint leaves (optional)

1. Prepare Cranberry Pineapple Smoothie Base.

2. In blender, combine 2 cups Smoothie Base and banana; process until smooth.

3. With blender running, add ice cubes, several at a time. Process until thick and smooth. If desired, garnish with orange peel and mint leaves.

Makes about 6 servings

Cranberry Pineapple Smoothie Base

1 cup KARO® Light Corn Syrup or KARO® Lite Syrup
1 can (16 ounces) whole berry cranberry sauce
1 can (8 ounces) crushed pineapple in unsweetened juice, undrained

In blender, combine all ingredients; process until smooth. Store covered in refrigerator up to 1 week.

Makes 4 cups

Prep Time: 10 minutes

Tropical Breeze Smoothie

1 cup frozen pineapple chunks

1 cup frozen mango chunks

½ cup unsweetened canned coconut milk

½ cup milk

2 tablespoons honey

1. Combine pineapple chunks, mango, coconut milk, milk and honey in blender; blend until smooth.

2. Pour into two glasses. Serve immediately. *Makes 2 servings*

Raspberry-Lemon Smoothie

1 cup frozen raspberries

1 container (6 ounces) lemon yogurt

½ cup milk

1 teaspoon vanilla

1. Combine raspberries, yogurt, milk and vanilla in blender; blend until smooth.

2. Pour into glass. Serve immediately. *Makes 1 serving*

Anti-Stress Smoothie

2 cups frozen blueberries

1 cup milk

1 cup vanilla frozen yogurt

1 medium banana

4 to 6 ice cubes

1 tablespoon honey

Whipped cream and lavender sprigs (optional)

1. Combine blueberries, milk, frozen yogurt, banana, ice and honey in blender; blend 1 minute or until mixture is frothy and ice is finely crushed.

2. Pour into four glasses. Garnish with whipped cream and lavender. Serve immediately.   *Makes 4 servings*

Note: Use unsprayed sprigs of lavender from the supermarket or floral shop.

Anti-Stress Smoothie

Strawberry Mango Smoothie

2 cups fresh or frozen strawberries, plus additional for garnish

1 cup fresh or frozen mango slices

¾ cup apricot juice

1 to 3 ice cubes

Fresh strawberries (optional)

1. Combine 2 cups strawberries, mango and apricot juice in blender; blend until smooth. Add 3 ice cubes if using fresh fruit and 1 to 2 ice cubes if using frozen fruit; blend until smooth.

2. Pour into two glasses. Garnish with additional strawberries. Serve immediately. *Makes 2 servings*

Pineapple Berry Smoothie

1 can (20 ounces) DOLE® Crushed Pineapple, undrained

1 cup vanilla nonfat yogurt

1 medium, ripe DOLE® Banana, quartered

1 cup DOLE® Pineapple Juice

½ cup DOLE® Fresh or Frozen Strawberries or Raspberries

½ cup ice cubes

• Combine crushed pineapple, yogurt, banana, pineapple juice, strawberries and ice cubes in blender or food processor container. Cover; blend until smooth. Garnish with strawberry and banana slice, if desired. *Makes 5 servings*

Prep Time: 5 minutes

Strawberry Mango Smoothies

Going Green

    1 cup green grapes
    ¼ honeydew melon, seeded and cut into chunks
    2 cups ice cubes
    4 kiwi, cut into quarters
    2 tablespoons honey
      Kiwi slices (optional)

1. Combine grapes, melon, ice, kiwi and honey in blender; blend until smooth.

2. Pour into four glasses. Garnish with kiwi slices. Serve immediately.

Makes 4 servings

Tropical Mango Strawberry Protein Smoothie

    ⅓ cup ALLWHITES®
    ¾ cup fresh or frozen strawberries
    ½ cup peeled chopped mango*
    1 container (6 ounces) low fat coconut cream pie yogurt
    ½ cup skim milk

Mango slices can be purchased in a jar in the produce section of your grocery store.

Combine all ingredients in blender. Cover and blend on medium speed until smooth. Serve immediately.

Makes 1 serving

Prep Time: 5 minutes

Tip: This recipe can be easily doubled.

Going Green

Mangorange Madness

    1 cup frozen sliced peaches
    1 cup frozen mango chunks
    ½ cup orange juice
    ½ cup plain yogurt
      Orange slices (optional)

1. Combine peaches, mango, orange juice and yogurt in blender; blend until smooth.

2. Pour into two glasses. Garnish with orange slices. Serve immediately.

Makes 2 servings

Papaya-Pineapple Smoothie

    ½ of 20-ounce can pineapple chunks in juice, drained and
      juice reserved
    2 cups papaya chunks
    1 to 2 tablespoons powdered sugar
    1 tablespoon lime juice

1. Place pineapple chunks in freezer 30 minutes or until frozen.

2. Combine frozen pineapple, reserved pineapple juice, papaya chunks, powdered sugar and lime juice in blender; blend until smooth.

3. Pour into two glasses. Serve immediately.

Makes 2 servings

Mangorange Madness

Mixed Berry Smoothie

1½ cups fresh or frozen strawberries

1 cup fresh or frozen blueberries

1 cup apple juice

1 container (6 ounces) mixed berry or vanilla yogurt

½ cup fresh or frozen raspberries

1 to 3 ice cubes

Fresh mint (optional)

1. Combine strawberries, blueberries, apple juice, yogurt and raspberries in blender; blend until smooth. Add 3 ice cubes if using fresh fruit or 1 to 2 ice cubes if using frozen fruit; blend until smooth.

2. Pour into two glasses. Garnish with mint. Serve immediately.

Makes 2 servings

Kiwi Pineapple Cream

1 cup frozen pineapple chunks

1 container (6 ounces) key lime yogurt

1 kiwi, peeled and sliced

½ cup canned unsweetened coconut milk

1 tablespoon honey

1. Combine pineapple, yogurt, kiwi, coconut milk and honey in blender; blend until smooth.

2. Pour into two glasses. Serve immediately. *Makes 2 servings*

Kiwi Chai Smoothie: Add ¼ teaspoon vanilla, ⅛ teaspoon cardamom, ⅛ teaspoon ground cinnamon, ⅛ teaspoon ground ginger and a pinch of cloves to the mixture before blending.

Mixed Berry Smoothies

Just for *Kids*

Strawberry Banana Coconut Smoothie

  2 cups fresh or frozen strawberries, plus additional for garnish
1¼ cups unsweetened canned coconut milk
  1 banana, sliced
  1 to 3 ice cubes

1. Combine 2 cups strawberries, coconut milk and banana in blender; blend until smooth. Add 3 ice cubes if using fresh fruit and 1 to 2 ice cubes if using frozen fruit; blend until smooth.

2. Pour into two glasses. Garnish with additional strawberries. Serve immediately.

Makes 2 servings

Peachy Banana Smoothie

1½ cups orange sherbet

1 package (16 ounces) frozen peaches *or* 2 cups
    sliced peeled fresh peaches

1 can (about 11 ounces) peach nectar

1 banana

1 cup ice cubes

Fresh mint (optional)

1. Combine sherbet, peaches, nectar, banana and ice in blender; blend until smooth.

2. Pour into four glasses. Garnish with mint. Serve immediately.

Makes 4 servings

Power Punch Smoothie

1 medium NC sweet potato

1 banana

1 cup crushed ice

1½ cups orange juice

2 tablespoons honey

1 cup plain yogurt

½ teaspoon cinnamon

1. Cook sweet potato in boiling water until tender. Cool, peel and mash to get 1 cup purée.

2. In blender, purée all ingredients until smooth and frothy. Serve cold.

Makes 2 servings

*Favorite recipe from **North Carolina SweetPotato Commission***

Peachy Banana Smoothies

Raspberry Chocolate Smoothie

2 cups fresh or frozen raspberries, plus additional for garnish

¾ cup milk

1 container (6 ounces) vanilla yogurt

3 tablespoons chocolate syrup

1 to 3 ice cubes

Whipped cream and chocolate shavings (optional)

1. Combine 2 cups raspberries, milk, yogurt and chocolate syrup in blender; blend until smooth. Add 3 ice cubes if using fresh fruit and 1 to 2 ice cubes if using frozen fruit; blend until smooth.

2. Pour into two glasses. Garnish with whipped cream, chocolate shavings and additional raspberries. Serve immediately.

Makes 2 servings

Honey Bear Smoothie

1 frozen banana

1 tablespoon honey

1 cup milk

¼ teaspoon cinnamon

¼ teaspoon vanilla

1. Combine banana, honey, milk, cinnamon and vanilla in blender; blend until smooth.

2. Pour into two glasses. Serve immediately.

Makes 2 servings

Raspberry Chocolate Smoothies

Nuts For Coconuts

1 tablespoon honey, divided

3 tablespoons sweetened coconut flakes, divided

1 cup coconut sorbet

½ cup coconut milk

¼ cup crushed ice

1. Dip rim of glass into ½ tablespoon honey and then into 1 tablespoon coconut flakes.

2. Combine sorbet, coconut milk, ice, remaining 2 tablespoons coconut flakes and ½ tablespoon honey in blender; blend until smooth.

3. Pour into prepared glass. Serve immediately.   *Makes 1 serving*

Cherry-Berry Smoothie

1 cup frozen whole unsweetened pitted dark sweet cherries

1 cup frozen whole unsweetened strawberries

1 cup cranberry-cherry juice

In blender, purée frozen pitted dark sweet cherries, frozen strawberries and juice, stirring as needed, until smooth.   *Makes 1 serving*

Note: Frozen pitted dark sweet cherries may be replaced with ¾ cup well-drained canned pitted dark sweet cherries and four ice cubes.

*Favorite recipe from **National Cherry Growers & Industries Foundation***

Nuts For Coconuts

Over the Rainbow

½ cup plus 1 tablespoon club soda, divided
  Colored sugar
1½ cups fruit punch
⅓ cup rainbow sherbet, plus additional for garnish

1. Wet rims of three glasses with 1 tablespoon soda, then dip into colored sugar.

2. Combine fruit punch and ⅓ cup sherbet in blender; blend until smooth.

3. Pour into prepared glasses; add club soda. Top with additional sherbet. Serve immediately. *Makes 3 servings*

Emerald City: Substitute green soft drink for fruit punch and lime sherbet for rainbow sherbet.

Yummy Fruit Smoothie

3 cups assorted fresh fruit (such as bananas, strawberries, mango, papaya, pineapple)
1 can (12 fluid ounces) NESTLÉ® CARNATION® Evaporated Milk, *chilled*
½ cup crushed ice
1 to 2 tablespoons sugar (optional)

PLACE fruit, evaporated milk and ice in blender; cover. Blend until smooth. Add sugar, if desired. *Makes 4 servings*

Variation: May substitute 3 cups cut-up frozen, unsweetened fruit or canned fruit for the fresh fruit. If using frozen fruit, thaw slightly and cut into smaller pieces. Crushed ice may not be needed. For canned fruit, drain and reserve juice or syrup. Substitute juice or syrup for sugar, if needed.

Over the Rainbow

Cinnamon-Apple Smoothie

2 cups ice cubes

2 apples, peeled and thinly sliced

2 bananas

1 container (6 ounces) vanilla yogurt

¾ cup apple juice

2 teaspoons ground cinnamon, plus additional for garnish

Whipped cream and unpeeled apple slices (optional)

1. Combine ice, 2 sliced apples, bananas, yogurt, apple juice and 2 teaspoons cinnamon in blender; blend until smooth.

2. Pour into four glasses. Top with whipped cream. Sprinkle with additional cinnamon. Garnish with apple slices. Serve immediately.

Makes 4 servings

To prepare this smoothie even quicker, use an apple corer/slicer. It is a wheel-shaped utensil that not only removes the core of an apple, but also cuts it into wedges. An apple corer will only remove the core, leaving the apple whole.

Cinnamon-Apple Smoothies

Cherry Cooler

4 cups orange juice

1½ cups cherries, pitted, plus additional for garnish

8 to 10 ice cubes

1 teaspoon vanilla

1. Combine orange juice, 1½ cups cherries, ice and vanilla in blender; blend until smooth.

2. Pour into four glasses. Garnish with additional cherries. Serve immediately. *Makes 4 servings*

Berry Blue Smoothie

2 cups fresh or slightly thawed frozen blueberries

1 container (8 ounces) low-fat vanilla yogurt

1 cup milk

1 can (6 ounces) unsweetened pineapple juice

3 tablespoons honey

1½ cups ice cubes (about 16 cubes)

In the container of an electric blender, place blueberries, yogurt, milk, pineapple juice and honey; blend until smooth. Add ice cubes, a few at a time, blend until finely crushed. Serve immediately.

Makes 4 servings

Favorite recipe from **U.S. Highbush Blueberry Council**

Cherry Coolers

Pour-It-On Peanut Butter Smoothie

2 cups vanilla frozen yogurt

2 bananas

2 cups ice cubes

1 cup milk

1 cup creamy peanut butter

2 tablespoons honey

1. Combine frozen yogurt, bananas, ice, milk, peanut butter and honey in blender; blend until smooth.

2. Pour into four glasses. Serve immediately.   *Makes 4 servings*

Gelatin Fruit Smoothie

2 cups strawberries

2 cups milk

1 package (4-serving size) strawberry gelatin

1. Combine strawberries, milk and gelatin in blender; blend until smooth and frothy.

2. Pour into four glasses. Serve immediately.   *Makes 4 servings*

Variation: Try your favorite gelatin and fruit combination.

Pour-It-On Peanut Butter Smoothies

Cherry Vanilla Chilla

2 ice cubes
¾ cup plain yogurt
¾ cup frozen cherries
½ cup milk
2 teaspoons sugar
1½ teaspoons vanilla

1. Crush ice in blender. Add yogurt, cherries, milk, sugar and vanilla; blend until smooth.

2. Pour into two glasses. Serve immediately.   *Makes 2 servings*

Chocolate Banana Peanut Butter Smoothie

1½ cups chocolate milk
2 tablespoons creamy peanut butter
1 medium ripe banana
2 cups vanilla yogurt
3 to 4 tablespoons sugar

1. Combine chocolate milk, peanut butter, banana, yogurt and sugar in blender; blend until smooth.

2. Pour into four glasses. Serve immediately.   *Makes 4 servings*

Purple Cow Jumped Over the Moon

  3 cups vanilla frozen yogurt

  1 cup milk

  ½ cup thawed frozen grape juice concentrate (undiluted)

  1½ teaspoons lemon juice

1. Combine yogurt, milk, juice concentrate and lemon juice in blender; blend until smooth.

2. Pour into eight glasses. Serve immediately.   *Makes 8 servings*

Razzmatazz Shake

  1 quart vanilla frozen yogurt

  1 cup vanilla yogurt

  ¼ cup chocolate syrup

  1 can (12 ounces) root beer

1. Combine frozen yogurt, yogurt and chocolate syrup in blender; blend until smooth.

2. Pour half of mixture into two glasses; top with half of root beer. Fill glasses equally with remaining yogurt mixture; top with remaining root beer. Serve immediately.   *Makes 12 servings*

Pumpkin Spice Smoothie

2½ cups vanilla frozen yogurt

1 cup solid-pack pumpkin

1 cup ice cubes

2 tablespoons packed brown sugar

1 tablespoon honey

1 teaspoon pumpkin pie spice

½ teaspoon ground nutmeg

1. Combine yogurt, pumpkin, ice, brown sugar, honey, pumpkin pie spice and nutmeg in blender; blend until smooth.

2. Pour into four glasses. Serve immediately. *Makes 4 servings*

Banana Blast Smoothie

1 cup Diet V8 SPLASH® Juice Drink, any flavor

½ cup plain nonfat yogurt

1 medium banana, sliced

2 ice cubes

1. Put all of the ingredients in a blender. Cover and blend until smooth.

Makes 2 servings

Prep Time: 5 minutes
Total Time: 5 minutes

Pumpkin Spice Smoothies

Raspberry Cocoa Freeze

½ cup fresh or frozen raspberries, plus additional for garnish

½ cup vanilla ice cream

⅓ cup milk

1 teaspoon unsweetened cocoa powder

Fresh mint (optional)

1. Combine ½ cup raspberries, ice cream, milk and cocoa in blender; blend until smooth.

2. Pour into two glasses. Garnish with additional raspberries and mint. Serve immediately.   *Makes 2 servings*

Lemon Mango Smoothie

¾ cup mango nectar

1 cup frozen mango chunks

¼ cup lemon sorbet

2 tablespoons fresh lime juice

1 to 2 tablespoons honey

¼ teaspoon lime peel

1. Combine nectar, mango, sorbet, lime juice, honey and lime peel in blender; blend until smooth.

2. Pour into glass. Serve immediately.   *Makes 1 serving*

Raspberry Cocoa Freeze

Wow Watermelon Smoothie

2 tablespoons sugar

4½ cups cubed seedless watermelon

1½ cups strawberry sorbet

1½ cups ice cubes

1 banana

1. Place sugar in small shallow dish. Wet rims of four glasses with damp paper towel; dip rims into sugar. Place glasses upright to dry.

2. Combine watermelon, sorbet, ice and banana in blender; blend until smooth.

3. Pour into prepared glasses. Serve immediately.   *Makes 4 servings*

Space Coast Smoothie

1 cup Florida grapefruit juice

½ cup vanilla yogurt

2 tablespoons mojito-flavored syrup*

4 ice cubes

Fresh mint leaves (optional)

Flavored syrups are available in supermarkets. Mint-flavored syrup can be substituted.

Combine grapefruit juice, yogurt, syrup and ice in blender; cover and blend until smooth. Pour into glass and garnish with mint leaf, if desired.

Makes 1 serving

*Favorite recipe from **Florida Department of Citrus***

Wow Watermelon Smoothies

Purpilicious Pomegranate Smoothie

½ **cup pomegranate juice**

⅓ **cup milk**

1 **cup frozen blueberries**

½ **cup raspberry sherbet**

1 **to 2 tablespoons honey**

1. Combine pomegranate juice, milk, blueberries, sherbet and honey in blender; blend until smooth.

2. Pour into glass. Serve immediately.   *Makes 1 serving*

Peanut Butter Banana Blend

1 **frozen banana**

½ **cup plain yogurt**

½ **cup milk**

1 **tablespoon all-natural, unsweetened peanut butter**

1. Combine frozen banana, yogurt, milk and peanut butter in blender; blend until smooth.

2. Pour into two glasses. Serve immediately.   *Makes 2 servings*

Purpilicious Pomegranate Smoothie

Light Lemon Strawberry Smoothie

   1 cup fresh or frozen strawberries, plus additional for garnish

   ¾ cup reduced-fat (2%) milk

   ½ cup plain fat-free yogurt

   1 tablespoon plus 1 teaspoon sugar

   1 tablespoon lemon juice

   Lemon wedges (optional)

1. Combine 1 cup strawberries, milk, yogurt, sugar and lemon juice in blender; blend until smooth.

2. Pour into two glasses. Garnish with lemon wedges and additional strawberries. Serve immediately. *Makes 2 servings*

Nutrients per Serving: Calories: 140, Total Fat: 2g, Saturated Fat: 1g, Cholesterol: 10mg, Sodium: 90mg, Carbohydrate: 25g, Fiber: 2g, Protein: 7g

Raspberry Soda Smoothie

2 cups fresh or frozen raspberries

1 can (12 ounces) ginger ale or lemon-lime soda

1 container (6 ounces) raspberry or vanilla yogurt

1 to 3 ice cubes

1. Combine raspberries, ginger ale and yogurt in blender; blend until smooth. Add 3 ice cubes if using fresh fruit or 1 to 2 ice cubes if using frozen fruit; blend until smooth.

2. Pour into two glasses. Serve immediately.

Makes 2 (12-ounce) servings

Nutrients per Serving: Calories: 166, Total Fat: 1g, Saturated Fat: 0g, Cholesterol: 1mg, Sodium: 51mg, Carbohydrate: 39g, Fiber: 8g, Protein: 4g

Variation: For a dairy-free alternative, add ½ cup raspberry sorbet and omit yogurt and ice cubes.

Raspberry Soda Smoothies

Honeydew Ginger Smoothie

1½ cups cubed honeydew melon

½ cup sliced banana

½ cup vanilla fat-free yogurt

½ cup ice cubes

¼ teaspoon grated fresh ginger

Honeydew melon balls and fresh ginger slices (optional)

1. Combine cubed honeydew, banana, yogurt, ice and grated ginger in blender; blend until smooth.

2. Pour into two glasses. Garnish with honeydew melon balls and ginger slices. Serve immediately. *Makes 2 (12-ounce) servings*

Nutrients per Serving: Calories: 70, Total Fat: 0g, Saturated Fat: 0g, Cholesterol: 0mg, Sodium: 35mg, Carbohydrate: 15g, Fiber: 1g, Protein: 2g

Cool & Creamy Fruit Smoothies

1 cup V8 SPLASH® Smoothies Strawberry Banana

½ cup peach sorbet or your favorite flavor

½ cup vanilla low-fat yogurt

½ cup fresh strawberries, cut into quarters

1. Put all of the ingredients in a blender. Cover and blend until smooth. Serve immediately. *Makes 2 servings*

Prep Time: 10 minutes
Total Time: 10 minutes

Nutrients per Serving: Calories: 173, Total Fat: 1g, Saturated Fat: 0g, Cholesterol: 1mg, Sodium: 70mg, Carbohydrate: 39g, Fiber: 2g, Protein: 4g

Honeydew Ginger Smoothies

Strawberry Kiwi Smoothie

2 kiwi
1 cup frozen whole strawberries
1 container (6 ounces) strawberry low-fat yogurt
½ cup low-fat (1%) milk
2 tablespoons honey

1. Combine kiwi, strawberries, yogurt, milk and honey in blender; blend until smooth.

2. Pour into four glasses. Serve immediately.

Makes 4 (½-cup) servings

Nutrients per Serving: Calories: 120, Total Fat: 1g, Saturated Fat: 0g, Cholesterol: 5mg, Sodium: 35mg, Carbohydrate: 27g, Fiber: 2g, Protein: 3g

Soy Strawberry Kiwi Smoothie: Substitute 1 container (6 ounces) strawberry soy yogurt for regular strawberry yogurt.

Strawberry Kiwi Smoothies

Green Tea Smoothie

½ cup boiling water

3 LIPTON® Green Tea with Mandarin Orange Flavor Pyramid Tea Bags

2 tablespoons sugar

½ cup BREYERS® Vanilla Frozen Yogurt or All Natural Vanilla Ice Cream

1 cup ice cubes (about 6 to 8)

Pour boiling water over LIPTON® Green Tea with Mandarin Orange Flavor Pyramid Tea Bags; cover and brew 5 minutes. Remove Tea Bags and squeeze, then stir in sugar; chill.

In blender, process tea with Ice Cream. Add ice cubes, one at a time, and process until blended. Serve immediately.   *Makes 2 servings*

Prep Time: 15 minutes
Brew Time: 5 minutes
Chill Time: 1 hour

Nutrients per Serving: Calories: 120, Total Fat: 3g, Saturated Fat: 2g, Cholesterol: 10mg, Sodium: 25mg, Carbohydrate: 24g, Fiber: 0g, Protein: 2g

Blackberry-Peach-Banana Smoothie

½ ripe medium banana

½ cup frozen sliced peaches, about 7 slices

1 (6-ounce) container plain fat-free yogurt

½ cup POLANER® Sugar Free Blackberry or Sugar Free Blueberry
    Preserves

¼ cup crushed ice

Place all ingredients in blender container. Cover; blend 1 to 2 minutes until smooth.

Serve immediately.   *Makes 2 servings (¾ cup per serving)*

Prep Time: 5 minutes

Nutrients per Serving: Calories: 126, Total Fat: >1g, Saturated Fat: >1g, Cholesterol: 2mg, Sodium: 66mg, Carbohydrate: 36g, Fiber: 1g, Protein: 5g

Tip: There is no need to thaw the frozen peaches. The icy texture helps give this smoothie a "creamy" thick consistency.

Serving Suggestion: Grab a few walnuts or almonds to eat along with your smoothie for a quick and healthy on-the-go snack.

Mandarin Orange Smoothie

1 can (11 ounces) mandarin orange sections, drained

1 cup orange sherbet

1 container (6 ounces) orange crème low-fat yogurt

½ cup orange juice or orange-tangerine juice, chilled

   Orange wedges (optional)

1. Combine orange sections, sherbet, yogurt and juice in blender; blend until nearly smooth.

2. Pour into three glasses. Garnish with orange wedges. Serve immediately.

Makes 3 (6-ounce) servings or 2¼ cups

Nutrients per Serving: Calories: 189, Total Fat: 2g, Saturated Fat: 1g, Cholesterol: 5mg, Sodium: 65mg, Carbohydrate: 39g, Fiber: 2g, Protein: 4g

Tip

When using oranges for juice, they should not be juiced until just before serving or there will be a significant loss in vitamin C. One large orange will yield about ½ cup of juice.

Mandarin Orange Smoothies

Fruity Smoothie

1 ripe large DOLE® Banana, peeled

1 can (8 ounces) DOLE® Pineapple Chunks, undrained

1 cup DOLE® Frozen Mixed Berries or Blueberries, partially thawed

1 carton (8 ounces) blueberry or mixed berry yogurt

• Slice banana into blender or food processor container. Add pineapple chunks, mixed berries and yogurt. Cover; blend until smooth.

Makes 3 servings

Prep Time: 5 minutes

Nutrients per Serving: Calories: 160, Total Fat: 1g, Saturated Fat: 0g, Cholesterol: 4mg, Sodium: 66mg, Carbohydrate: 36g, Fiber: 2g, Protein: 3g

Variations: Replace 1 cup mixed berries and blueberry yogurt with 1 cup DOLE® Frozen Sliced Peaches and peach yogurt, 1 cup DOLE® Frozen Raspberries and mixed berry yogurt or 1 cup DOLE® Frozen Strawberries and strawberry yogurt.

Fruity Smoothies

Raspberry Smoothie

1½ cups fresh or frozen raspberries, plus additional for garnish

1 cup plain sugar-free fat-free yogurt

2 packets sugar substitute *or* equivalent of 4 teaspoons sugar

1 tablespoon honey

1 to 3 ice cubes

Fresh mint (optional)

1. Combine 1½ cups raspberries, yogurt, sugar substitute and honey in blender; blend until smooth. Add 3 ice cubes if using fresh fruit or 1 to 2 ice cubes if using frozen fruit; blend until smooth.

2. Pour into two glasses. Garnish with additional raspberries and mint. Serve immediately. *Makes 2 (1½-cup) servings*

Nutrients per Serving: Calories: 143, Total Fat: <1g, Saturated Fat: <1g, Cholesterol: 2mg, Sodium: 88mg, Carbohydrate: 28g, Fiber: 6g, Protein: 8g

Peachy Keen Smoothie

2 cups frozen sliced peaches

1 container (6 ounces) peach low-fat yogurt

½ cup reduced-fat (2%) milk

¼ teaspoon vanilla

1. Combine peaches, yogurt, milk and vanilla in blender; blend until smooth.

2. Pour into two glasses. Serve immediately. *Makes 2 servings*

Nutrients per Serving: Calories: 170, Total Fat: 2g, Saturated Fat: 2g, Cholesterol: 10mg, Sodium: 85mg, Carbohydrate: 34g, Fiber: 2g, Protein: 7g

Raspberry Smoothie

Mango Smoothie

2 cups frozen mango cubes*

2 containers (6 ounces each) vanilla low-fat yogurt

¾ cup orange juice

1 teaspoon vanilla (optional)

Juice of ½ lime

Pinch salt

Mango wedges (optional)

You can find frozen mango cubes in the supermarket near the other frozen fruit.

1. Combine mango, yogurt, orange juice, vanilla, if desired, lime juice and salt in blender; blend until smooth.

2. Pour into four glasses. Garnish with mango wedges. Serve immediately.

Makes 4 (5-ounce) servings

Nutrients per Serving: Calories: 93, Total Fat: <1g, Saturated Fat: 0g, Cholesterol: 1mg, Sodium: 39mg, Carbohydrate: 21g, Fiber: 1g, Protein: 3g

 *Tip*

Mangoes are an excellent source of vitamin A and are a very good source of vitamin C. They also provide potassium and fiber, and they're sodium-free. If you can't find frozen mango cubes, you can make your own. Cut 1 mango into 1-inch chunks; place on a cookie sheet and freeze for about 3 hours.

Mango Smoothie

Red Tea Harvest Strawberry Smoothie

1 cup boiling water

3 LIPTON® Red Tea with Harvest Strawberry & Passionfruit Flavor
    Pyramid Tea Bags

2 tablespoons sugar

1 cup frozen strawberries

½ cup strawberry frozen yogurt*

½ cup ice cubes (about 3 to 4)

You may use regular strawberry yogurt.

Pour boiling water over LIPTON® Red Tea with Harvest Strawberry & Passionfruit Flavor Pyramid Tea Bags; cover and brew 5 minutes. Remove Tea Bags and squeeze, then stir in sugar; chill.

In blender, process tea, strawberries and yogurt. Add ice cubes, one at a time, and process until blended. Garnish, if desired, with whipped cream and strawberries. Serve immediately.   *Makes 2 servings*

Chill Time: 1 hour

Nutrients per Serving: Calories: 130, Total Fat: 1g, Saturated Fat: 0g, Cholesterol: 5mg, Sodium: 35mg, Carbohydrate: 29g, Fiber: 2g, Protein: 3g

Variation: For a twist, stir in ¼ cup rum.

Pumpkin Pie Smoothie

1 can (15 ounces) LIBBY'S® 100% Pure Pumpkin, *chilled*

1 can (12 fluid ounces) NESTLÉ® CARNATION® Evaporated Fat Free
Milk, *chilled*

1 cup crushed ice

⅔ cup (6 ounces) vanilla light and nonfat yogurt

¼ cup granulated sugar

¼ teaspoon pumpkin pie spice

Light whipped cream

COMBINE pumpkin, evaporated milk, ice, yogurt, sugar and pumpkin pie spice in blender; cover. Blend until mixture is smooth. If a thinner smoothie is desired, add water, a little at a time, until desired consistency is reached.

TOP with whipped cream; sprinkle with additional pumpkin pie spice.

Makes 5 servings

Prep Time: 3 minutes

Nutrients per Serving: Calories: 180, Total Fat: 4g, Saturated Fat: 3g, Cholesterol: 15mg, Sodium: 110mg, Carbohydrate: 28g, Fiber: 3g, Protein: 8g

Note: For a richer and creamier version of this recipe, substitute NESTLÉ® CARNATION® Evaporated Lowfat 2% Milk or Evaporated Milk for the Evaporated Fat Free Milk.

Spiced Passion Fruit-Yogurt Smoothie

- 1 cup plain fat-free yogurt
- 1 cup sliced strawberries
- 1 ripe banana, sliced
- ¼ cup frozen passion fruit juice concentrate or frozen apple-passion-mango fruit juice concentrate, thawed
- ¾ teaspoon pumpkin pie spice
- ⅛ teaspoon ground white pepper

1. Combine yogurt, strawberries, banana, juice concentrate, pumpkin pie spice and white pepper in blender; blend until smooth.

2. Pour into three glasses. Serve immediately.

Makes 3 (6-ounce) servings or 2⅓ cups

Nutrients per Serving: Calories: 110, Total Fat: <1g, Saturated Fat: 0g, Cholesterol: 0mg, Sodium: 65mg, Carbohydrate: 23g, Fiber: 2g, Protein: 6g

Spiced Passion Fruit-Yogurt Smoothie

Soy Milk Smoothie

3 cups plain or vanilla soy milk

1 banana, peeled and frozen (see Tip)

1 cup frozen strawberries or raspberries

1 teaspoon vanilla or almond extract

⅓ cup EQUAL® SPOONFUL*

May substitute 8 packets EQUAL® sweetener.

• Place all ingredients in blender or food processor. Blend until smooth.

Makes 4 servings

Nutrients per Serving: Calories: 147, Total Fat: 3g, Saturated Fat: <1g, Cholesterol: 0mg, Sodium: 92mg, Carbohydrate: 18g, Fiber: 2g, Protein: 6g

Tip: Peel and cut banana into large chunks. Place in plastic freezer bag, seal and freeze at least 5 to 6 hours or overnight.

Pineberry Smoothie

1 ripe DOLE® Banana, quartered

1 cup DOLE® Pineapple Juice

½ cup nonfat vanilla or plain yogurt

½ cup DOLE® Frozen Strawberries, Raspberries or Blueberries

• Combine all ingredients in blender or food processor container. Blend until thick and smooth. Serve immediately.

Makes 2 servings

Prep Time: 5 minutes

Nutrients per Serving: Calories: 175, Total Fat: 1g, Saturated Fat: <1g, Cholesterol: 0mg, Sodium: 36mg, Carbohydrate: 41g, Fiber: 2g, Protein: 3g

Soy Milk Smoothies

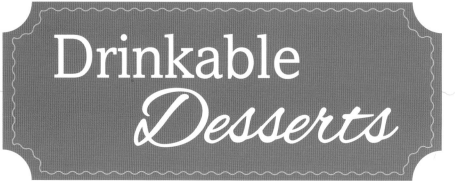

Banana Split Smoothie

1 banana

¾ cup milk

1 tablespoon strawberry syrup

1 tablespoon chocolate syrup

Whipped cream (optional)

1 maraschino cherry (optional)

Candy sprinkles (optional)

1. Peel banana, cut into chunks and seal in plastic wrap. Place wrapped banana in freezer until frozen, about 2 hours. (Banana may be frozen up to 2 weeks ahead of time.)

2. Place frozen banana chunks and milk in blender; blend until smooth. Pour about one-third of mixture into tall glass. Add strawberry syrup to remaining mixture in blender; blend just until combined. Pour about half of strawberry mixture over banana mixture in glass.

3. Add chocolate syrup to remaining mixture in blender; blend until smooth. Pour on top of strawberry mixture in glass. Top with whipped cream, cherry and sprinkles. Serve immediately.   *Makes 1 serving*

Berry Berry Mango Smoothie

1 medium mango, cubed

1 cup fresh or frozen strawberries, plus additional for garnish

½ cup fresh or frozen raspberries, plus additional for garnish

½ cup low fat vanilla yogurt

½ cup milk

2 tablespoons honey

Mango wedges (optional)

1. Combine mango, 1 cup strawberries, ½ cup raspberries, yogurt, milk and honey in blender; blend until smooth.

2. Pour into two glasses. Garnish with mango wedges, additional strawberries and raspberries. Serve immediately. *Makes 2 servings*

Watermelon Yogurt Mint Smoothie

1 to 2 cups seedless watermelon chunks

1 tablespoon honey

1 tablespoon fresh mint leaves or to taste

1 cup lemon yogurt

Dash cinnamon

Combine watermelon, honey and mint in blender. Purée, being careful not to over-blend; there should be some texture left to mixture. Add yogurt and cinnamon and pulse just until smooth.

Makes 1 to 2 servings

*Favorite recipe from **National Watermelon Promotion Board***

Berry Berry Mango Smoothie

Carrot Cake Smoothie

4 jars (4 ounces each) baby food carrots

1 cup vanilla low-fat frozen yogurt

½ cup milk

¼ cup sugar

2 ice cubes

½ teaspoon ground cinnamon

⅛ teaspoon ground ginger

   Dash ground nutmeg

   Dash salt

4 carrots (optional)

1. Combine baby food, frozen yogurt, milk, sugar, ice, cinnamon, ginger, nutmeg and salt in blender; blend until smooth.

2. Pour into four glasses. Garnish with carrots. Serve immediately.

Makes 4 servings

Tip

A dash refers to a very small amount of a dry or liquid ingredient, most often a seasoning. Although it is not an exact measure, a dash is generally more than ¹⁄₁₆ and less than ⅛ of a teaspoon.

Carrot Cake Smoothies

"Hot" Chocolate Smoothie

2½ cups chocolate low-fat frozen yogurt
1¾ cups chocolate soymilk
1½ cups ice cubes
1 banana
⅛ teaspoon chipotle chili powder
Whipped cream and chocolate shavings (optional)

1. Combine frozen yogurt, soymilk, ice, banana and chili powder in blender; blend until smooth.

2. Pour into four glasses. Top with whipped cream and chocolate shavings. Serve immediately. *Makes 4 servings*

Strawberry Frozen Yogurt Smoothie

1 cup boiling water
3 LIPTON® Cup Size Tea Bags *or* 1 LIPTON® Iced Tea Brew Family Size
  Tea Bag
1 pint strawberries, hulled
1 cup BREYERS® All Natural Frozen Vanilla Yogurt or Ice Cream
2 tablespoons sugar
1 cup ice cubes (about 6 to 8)

In teapot, pour boiling water over LIPTON® Cup Size Tea Bags; cover and brew 5 minutes. Remove Tea Bags; cool slightly.

In blender, combine tea, strawberries, yogurt and sugar. Add ice cubes, one at a time, and process until blended. Serve immediately.

Makes 3 servings

"Hot" Chocolate Smoothies

Lemon Chiffon Cooler

2 cups milk

2 cups (1 pint) lemon sorbet, softened

1 cup French vanilla ice cream, softened

2 teaspoons grated lemon peel, plus additional for garnish

⅓ cup lemon juice

1 tablespoon sugar

Whipped cream (optional)

1. Combine milk, sorbet, ice cream, 2 teaspoons lemon peel, lemon juice and sugar in blender; blend until smooth.

2. Pour into four glasses. Top each glass with whipped cream and sprinkle with additional lemon peel. Serve immediately.   *Makes 4 servings*

When grating lemon peel, be sure to use only the yellow part of the peel and not the bitter white part. Grate the peel before you juice the lemon.

Lemon Chiffon Coolers

Tiramisu Smoothie

8 ounces mascarpone cheese

¾ cup vanilla frozen yogurt

¼ cup half-and-half

1½ cups chocolate frozen yogurt

½ cup brewed espresso or strong coffee, chilled

1 tablespoon powdered sugar

1 tablespoon cocoa powder

Pirouette cookies or thin biscotti (optional)

1. Combine mascarpone, vanilla frozen yogurt and half-and-half in blender; blend until smooth. Pour mixture into bowl or pitcher; set aside.

2. Combine chocolate frozen yogurt and espresso in blender; blend until smooth.

3. Pour into four glasses. Top chocolate mixture with mascarpone mixture.

4. Mix powdered sugar and cocoa in small bowl. Sift mixture into each glass. Garnish with pirouette cookies. Serve immediately.

Makes 4 servings

Tiramisu Smoothies

Piña Colada Smoothie

½ cup Piña Colada Smoothie Base (recipe follows)

1 small ripe banana

1 cup pineapple juice

4 cups ice cubes

¾ cup rum (optional)

Fresh fruit (optional)

1. Prepare Piña Colada Smoothie Base.

2. In blender combine ½ cup Smoothie Base with banana and pineapple juice; process until smooth.

3. With blender running, add ice cubes, several at a time, then rum. Blend until thickened and smooth. If desired, garnish with fresh fruit.

Makes about 6 servings

Piña Colada Smoothie Base

1 cup KARO® Light Corn Syrup

1 can (15 ounces) cream of coconut

1 can (8 ounces) crushed pineapple in unsweetened juice, undrained

¼ cup lime juice

In blender combine all ingredients; process until smooth. Store covered in refrigerator up to 1 week.

Makes 3½ cups

Prep Time: 10 minutes

Blueberry Cherry "Cheesecake" Smoothie

2 cups fresh or frozen blueberries
1¼ cups milk
½ cup fresh or frozen cherries
¼ cup (2 ounces) cream cheese
1 to 3 ice cubes

1. Combine blueberries, milk, cherries and cream cheese in blender; blend until smooth. Add 3 ice cubes if using fresh fruit and 1 to 2 ice cubes if using frozen fruit; blend until smooth.

2. Pour into two glasses. Serve immediately.   *Makes 2 servings*

Black Forest Smoothie

1 container (6 ounces) dark cherry yogurt
½ cup frozen dark sweet cherries
¼ cup milk
1 to 2 ice cubes
2 tablespoons sugar
2 tablespoons unsweetened cocoa powder
¼ teaspoon almond extract

1. Combine yogurt, cherries, milk, ice, sugar, cocoa and almond extract in blender; blend until smooth.

2. Pour into two glasses. Serve immediately.   *Makes 2 servings*

Dreamsicle Smoothie

2 cups ice cubes

1½ cups vanilla yogurt

¾ cup frozen orange juice concentrate

½ cup milk

¼ teaspoon vanilla

Whipped cream and orange slices (optional)

1. Combine ice, yogurt, juice concentrate, milk and vanilla in blender; blend until smooth.

2. Pour into four glasses. Garnish with whipped cream and orange slices. Serve immediately. *Makes 4 servings*

Dessert Date Smoothie

½ cup (about 10) dried pitted dates

2 scoops vanilla ice cream or frozen yogurt

1 tablespoon honey

⅛ teaspoon ground nutmeg

1. Place dates in microwaveable glass measuring cup. Add enough water to equal ½ cup. Microwave on HIGH 1 minute; allow to cool to room temperature, about 15 minutes.

2. Place undrained dates in blender with ice cream, honey and ⅛ teaspoon nutmeg; blend until smooth.

3. Pour into tall glass. Serve immediately. *Makes 1 serving*

Dreamsicle Smoothies

Banana-Coconut "Cream Pie" Smoothie

3 bananas, cut into chunks

1½ cups unsweetened canned coconut milk, chilled*

1½ cups pineapple juice, chilled

3 ice cubes

2 tablespoons sugar

½ teaspoon vanilla

⅛ teaspoon ground nutmeg

Shredded sweetened coconut, toasted (optional)**

*Do not use coconut cream, which is a sweetened product used for alcoholic beverages.
**To toast coconut, spread in single layer in heavy skillet. Cook over medium heat 1 to 2 minutes or until lightly browned, stirring frequently.

1. Combine bananas, coconut milk, pineapple juice, ice, sugar, vanilla and nutmeg in blender; blend until smooth.

2. Pour into four glasses. Garnish with toasted coconut. Serve immediately.

Makes 4 servings

Note: If desired, combine the ingredients in a large pitcher and blend using an immersion blender.

Banana-Coconut "Cream Pie" Smoothies

Strawberry Sundae Smoothie

   3 cups ice cubes

10 ounces frozen unsweetened strawberries, thawed

   1 cup milk

¾ cup plain yogurt

   2 bananas

   2 tablespoons sugar

    Whipped cream and chocolate syrup (optional)

    Candy sprinkles or nonpareils (optional)

1. Combine ice, strawberries, milk, yogurt, bananas and sugar in blender; blend until ice is crushed.

2. Pour into four glasses. Top with whipped cream, chocolate syrup and sprinkles. Serve immediately.

Makes 4 servings

Irresistible Peach Smoothies

   2 cups peeled, pitted and diced fresh Washington peaches

½ cup lowfat milk

   1 cup vanilla ice cream

   1 tablespoon fresh lemon juice

Combine all ingredients in blender container and blend until smooth.

Makes 3 servings

Tip: For a super cold smoothie, layer diced peaches in a single layer on a freezer-safe pan and freeze 1 hour or until completely frozen.

*Favorite recipe from **Washington State Fruit Commission***

Strawberry Sundae Smoothies

S'mores Amore Smoothie

1 cup French vanilla ice cream

1 cup chocolate ice cream

½ cup milk

2 to 3 ice cubes

¼ cup mini marshmallows

¼ cup mini semisweet chocolate chips

1 graham cracker, divided

Whipped cream (optional)

1. Combine vanilla ice cream, chocolate ice cream, milk and ice in blender; blend until smooth. Add marshmallows, chocolate chips and half of graham cracker; blend just until combined.

2. Pour into two chilled glasses. Crush remaining graham cracker half. Top smoothies with whipped cream and crushed cracker crumbs. Serve immediately.

Makes 2 servings

S'mores Amore Smoothies

Lemon Melon Crème Smoothie

Crushed lemon candies
½ of a 12-ounce can frozen lemonade concentrate, thawed
3 cups honeydew melon chunks
2 tablespoons vanilla yogurt
Candied lemon slices (optional)

1. Place crushed candies into small shallow dish. Wet rims of three glasses with damp paper towel; dip rims into candy.

2. Pour half of lemonade concentrate into blender. Add honeydew melon, remaining concentrate and yogurt; blend until smooth.

3. Pour into prepared glasses. Garnish with candied lemon slices. Serve immediately. *Makes 3 servings*

Banana Pudding Smoothie

1 medium banana, frozen
¾ cup milk
1 tablespoon packed light brown sugar
2 teaspoons vanilla extract

1. Break frozen banana into chunks. Place banana, milk, brown sugar and vanilla in blender; blend until smooth.

2. Pour into glass. Serve immediately. *Makes 1 serving*

Lemon Melon Crème Smoothies

Key Lime Pie Refresher

1 graham cracker, finely crushed

2 cups ice cubes

1 can (14 ounces) sweetened condensed milk

1 cup half-and-half

1 tablespoon grated lime peel

1 cup key lime juice

   Whipped cream and lime slices (optional)

1. Place cracker crumbs into small shallow dish. Wet rims of four glasses with damp paper towel; dip rims into crumbs.

2. Combine ice, sweetened condensed milk, half-and-half, lime peel and lime juice in blender; blend until smooth.

3. Pour into prepared glasses. Garnish with whipped cream and lime slices. Serve immediately.   *Makes 4 servings*

Mint-Caramel Tornado

1½ cups chocolate frozen yogurt

¾ cup vanilla frozen yogurt

¾ cup milk

¼ cup caramel ice cream topping

¼ cup mint chocolate chips

1. Combine frozen yogurts, milk, ¼ cup caramel topping and ¼ cup mint chocolate chips in blender; blend until smooth.

2. Pour into four glasses. Serve immediately.   *Makes 4 servings*

Key Lime Pie Refreshers

Shake It *Up*

Horchata Shake

2 cups rice milk or milk

1 cup well-cooked rice*

1 cup vanilla ice cream

4 ice cubes

¼ cup sugar

½ teaspoon cinnamon

½ teaspoon vanilla

¼ teaspoon salt

Rice should be soft enough to mash with a fork.

1. Combine rice milk, rice, ice cream, ice, sugar, cinnamon, vanilla and salt in blender; blend until frothy and ice is finely ground.

2. Strain mixture into pitcher. Discard solids. Serve immediately or chill for several hours. Stir well before serving.   *Makes 4 servings*

Red Velvet Shake

2 (1-ounce) squares white chocolate

2 tablespoons maraschino cherry juice

¾ cup milk

8 maraschino cherries

½ cup raspberry sherbet

4 to 8 drops red food coloring

Whipped topping (optional)

Semisweet chocolate curls (optional)

1. Microwave chocolate and cherry juice in microwavable bowl on HIGH 30 seconds. Stir. If necessary, microwave at 10-second intervals, stirring until chocolate is completely melted and mixture is smooth.

2. Place milk and cherries in blender; blend until smooth. Add chocolate mixture; blend until smooth. Add sherbet and food coloring; blend until smooth.

3. Pour into two glasses. Garnish with whipped topping and chocolate curls. Serve immediately. *Makes 2 servings*

Note: ½ cup vanilla low-fat frozen yogurt may be substituted for sherbet.

Red Velvet Shake

TOLL HOUSE® Chocolate Chip Cookie Milkshake

1 pint (2 cups) vanilla ice cream

2 cups (about 8) freshly baked and crumbled NESTLÉ® TOLL HOUSE® Refrigerated Chocolate Chip Cookies

1 cup milk *or* ⅔ cup (5-ounce can) NESTLÉ® CARNATION® Evaporated Milk, chilled

PLACE ice cream, cookies and 1 cup milk *or* ⅔ cup (5-ounce can) NESTLÉ® CARNATION® Evaporated Milk in blender; cover. Blend until smooth. If a smoother shake is desired, add some additional milk.

Makes 3 servings

Prep Time: 5 minutes

Creamy Pineapple Shake

1 can (20 ounces) DOLE® Crushed Pineapple, undrained

1 pint vanilla ice cream or frozen yogurt

1 cup milk

Dash ground cinnamon

• Combine crushed pineapple, ice cream, milk and cinnamon in blender or food processor container. Cover; blend until smooth.

Makes 4 servings

Prep Time: 5 minutes

TOLL HOUSE® Chocolate Chip Cookie Milkshake

Beat-the-Heat Tea Shake

4 cups boiling water

6 LIPTON® Cup Size Tea Bags

2 cups (1 pint) BREYERS® SMOOTH AND DREAMY™ Ice Cream OR sherbet, any flavor

    Fresh strawberries (optional)

Pour boiling water over LIPTON® Cup Size Tea Bags; cover and brew 5 minutes. Remove Tea Bags and squeeze; chill tea.

Process 2½ cups tea with BREYERS® SMOOTH AND DREAMY™ Ice Cream in blender at high speed until blended. Garnish, if desired, with strawberries. *Makes 4 servings*

Iced Tea Float: For another cool, refreshing summer treat, whip up an Iced Tea Float. Put a scoop of frozen yogurt into a tall glass. Pour in ice-cold brewed tea made with LIPTON® Green Tea with Mandarin Orange Flavor Pyramid Tea Bags. Top the float with a splash of seltzer.

Prep Time: 10 minutes
Brew Time: 5 minutes
Chill Time: 15 minutes

Maraschino Cherry Shake

1 (10-ounce) jar maraschino cherries

3 tablespoons maraschino cherry juice

3 cups vanilla ice cream

Whipped topping

Whole maraschino cherries, for garnish

Put a colander or strainer in a bowl. Pour cherries into the strainer. Measure out 3 tablespoons of juice and put it in a small container. (You can either discard the remaining juice or save it for another use.)

Put cherries from the strainer on a cutting board. With a sharp knife, carefully cut cherries into small pieces.

Put chopped cherries, 3 tablespoons juice and ice cream in the container of an electric blender or food processor; cover blender. Process or blend until smooth.

Pour into 2 (12-ounce) glasses. Top with whipped topping; garnish with whole maraschino cherries.   *Makes 2 servings*

Favorite recipe from **Cherry Marketing Institute**

Piña Colada Milkshake

2 cups (1 pint) coconut sorbet

2 cups (1 pint) vanilla frozen yogurt or ice cream

¾ cup pineapple juice

¼ cup dark rum

Pineapple wedges (optional)

1. Combine sorbet, frozen yogurt, pineapple juice and rum in blender; blend until smooth.

2. Pour into four glasses. Garnish with pineapple wedges. Serve immediately. *Makes 4 servings*

Purple Power Shake

1½ cups vanilla low-fat frozen yogurt

¼ to ½ cup 100% grape juice

1 teaspoon lemon juice (optional)

1. Combine frozen yogurt, grape juice and lemon juice, if desired, in blender; blend until smooth.

2. Pour into four glasses. Serve immediately. *Makes 4 servings*

Sunshine Shake: Combine 2 cups (1 pint) vanilla frozen yogurt, ⅔ cup orange juice, ½ cup fresh or thawed frozen raspberries and ½ teaspoon sugar in blender; blend until smooth. Pour into five glasses. Sprinkle with ground nutmeg. Serve immediately. *Makes 5 servings*

Piña Colada Milkshakes

Pumpkin Pie Milkshake

1 cup canned pumpkin pie mix

1 cup milk

½ teaspoon vanilla

4 cups vanilla ice cream

4 graham cracker squares, plus additional for garnish

Whipped cream (optional)

1. Combine pumpkin pie mix, milk and vanilla in blender; blend until smooth. Add ice cream; blend until smooth. Add 4 graham crackers; blend just until small chunks remain.

2. Pour into four glasses. Garnish with whipped cream and additional graham crackers. Serve immediately. *Makes 4 servings*

Cantaloupe Strawberry Shake

1 cup hulled strawberries

1 cup cubed cantaloupe

⅔ cup skim milk

2 teaspoons sugar

Add ingredients to food processor or blender. Process until smooth and frothy. Serve immediately. *Makes 2 servings*

*Favorite recipe from **The Sugar Association, Inc.***

Pumpkin Pie Milkshakes

Chocolate Chocolate Cookie Shake

1¼ cups crushed mini crème-filled cookies (about 3 cups cookies), divided

⅓ cup cold milk, divided

⅛ teaspoon ground cinnamon

1¼ cups vanilla ice cream

¼ cup mini semisweet chocolate chips

Whipped cream (optional)

Mini crème-filled cookies (optional)

1. Combine ½ cup cookie crumbs and 1 tablespoon milk, mixing with fork until blended. Press 2 tablespoons crumb mixture into bottom of three 4-ounce glasses; reserve remaining crumb mixture. Place glasses in freezer.

2. Combine cinnamon with ½ cup of reserved cookie crumbs. Place remaining milk, cinnamon crumb mixture, ice cream and semisweet chocolate chips in blender; blend until smooth.

3. Pour chocolate mixture over cookie base in prepared glasses. Garnish with whipped cream, reserved crumb mixture and mini cookies. Serve immediately.   *Makes about 3 servings*

Chocolate Chocolate Cookie Shakes

Christmas in July

1 cup vanilla ice cream or frozen yogurt

1 cup peppermint ice cream

½ cup milk

3 or 4 ice cubes

2 candy canes broken into 3 or 4 pieces

2 tablespoons white chocolate chips

Whipped cream, candy cane pieces and whole candy canes (optional)

1. Place vanilla ice cream, peppermint ice cream, milk, ice, broken candy canes and white chocolate chips in blender; blend until smooth.

2. Pour mixture into two glasses. Garnish with whipped cream, candy cane pieces and whole candy canes. Serve immediately.

Makes 2 servings

Peanut Butter Chocolate Twist Shake

6 ounces frozen vanilla yogurt or ice cream

½ cup (4 ounces) canned unsweetened coconut milk

1 ounce chocolate chips

1 ounce peanut butter

2 curls shaved chocolate

½ ounce crushed roasted peanuts

Whip all ingredients except shaved chocolate and peanuts together in blender until smooth. Garnish with shaved chocolate and crushed roasted peanuts.

Makes 1 serving

*Favorite recipe from **Peanut Advisory Board***

Christmas in July

Mango Milk Shakes

2 cups V8 V-FUSION® Peach Mango Juice or V8 SPLASH® Tropical Blend Juice Drink

1 cup vanilla ice cream

1. Put the juice and ice cream in a blender. Cover and blend until the mixture is smooth. Serve immediately. *Makes 2 servings*

Prep Time: 5 minutes
Total Time: 5 minutes

Frosty Five-Spice Coffee Shake

1 cup ice cubes

⅓ cup vanilla ice cream or frozen yogurt

2 tablespoons sweetened condensed milk

1 tablespoon instant coffee powder or granules

¼ teaspoon Chinese five-spice powder

1. Combine ice, ice cream, sweetened condensed milk, coffee powder and five-spice powder in blender; blend until smooth.

2. Pour into glass. Serve immediately. *Makes 1 serving*

Mango Milk Shakes

Mint Chocolate Chip Milkshakes

2 cups mint chocolate chip ice cream

1 cup milk

2 tablespoons whipped topping (optional)

1 tablespoon mini chocolate chips (optional)

1. Combine ice cream and milk in blender; blend until smooth.

2. Pour into two glasses. Top with whipped topping; sprinkle with chocolate chips. Serve immediately. *Makes 2 servings*

Cocoa-Nut Shake

1½ cups vanilla ice cream

½ cup coconut milk

1 teaspoon cocoa powder

2 tablespoons sweetened coconut flakes, plus additional for garnish

1. Combine ice cream, coconut milk, cocoa and 2 tablespoons coconut in blender; blend until smooth.

2. Pour into two glasses. Sprinkle with coconut flakes. Serve immediately.

Makes 2 servings

Mint Chocolate Chip Milkshakes

Root Beer Barrel Shake

1 scoop vanilla ice cream or frozen yogurt

1 cup root beer

½ teaspoon root beer extract

Whipped cream (optional)

Root beer-flavored hard candy, crushed (optional)

1. Place glass mug in freezer at least 1 hour before serving time, if desired.

2. Combine ice cream, root beer and root beer extract in blender; blend until smooth.

3. Pour in frozen mug. Top with whipped cream and candies. Serve immediately.   *Makes 1 serving*

Note: Most grocery stores sell root beer extract in the baking aisle by the spices, extracts and flavorings.

Dreamy Banana Shakes

2 cups BREYERS® All Natural Chocolate or Vanilla Ice Cream

½ cup SKIPPY® Creamy Peanut Butter

½ cup milk

1 medium banana

Process all ingredients in blender until smooth. Serve immediately.

Makes 2 servings

Prep Time: 10 minutes

Root Beer Barrel Shakes

Frozen Hot Chocolate

½ **cup milk**

3 **tablespoons sugar**

3 **ounces finely chopped semisweet chocolate** *or* ⅔ **cup semisweet chocolate chips**

1 **tablespoon hot chocolate mix**

4 **scoops chocolate ice cream**

2 **cups ice cubes**

Whipped cream and chocolate sprinkles or mini marshmallows (optional)

1. Combine milk, sugar, chopped chocolate and hot chocolate mix in medium microwavable bowl. Microwave on HIGH 30 seconds; stir until chocolate is melted and mixture is smooth. Cool to room temperature, about 1 hour (or refrigerate and bring to room temperature when ready to serve).

2. Place chocolate mixture, ice cream and ice in blender; blend until smooth.

3. Pour into four glasses. Garnish with whipped cream and sprinkles. Serve immediately. *Makes 4 servings*

Frozen Hot Chocolate

Summer Drinks

Sparkling Pomegranate Gingerade

½ cup sugar

¼ cup water

1 teaspoon grated lemon peel

1 (1-inch) piece fresh ginger, thinly sliced

2 cups seltzer water

2 cups pomegranate juice

Ice cubes

Fresh mint (optional)

1. Combine sugar, water, lemon peel and ginger in small saucepan over medium heat; bring mixture to a boil. Boil 1 minute. Remove from heat; cool completely.

2. Strain syrup into large pitcher; discard solids. Stir in seltzer water and pomegranate juice.

3. Pour mixture over ice into four glasses. Garnish with mint. Serve immediately. *Makes 4 servings*

Thai Coconut Iced Tea

2 bags jasmine tea

2 cups boiling water

1 cup unsweetened canned coconut milk

2 tablespoons sugar, divided

Ice cubes

Lemon slices and fresh mint (optional)

1. Brew 2 cups tea with boiling water according to package directions; cool to room temperature.

2. Divide coconut milk and sugar between two glasses; stir until dissolved. Add ice.

3. Carefully pour half of tea into prepared glasses. Garnish with lemon and mint. Serve immediately.   *Makes 2 servings*

Strawberry Limeade

1½ cups quartered fresh strawberries

1 cup lime juice

4 cups water

1½ cups EQUAL® SPOONFUL*

6 small whole strawberries or lime wedges (optional)

*May substitute 36 packets EQUAL® sweetener.

• Blend strawberries and lime juice in blender or food processor until smooth. Combine strawberry mixture, water and Equal® in pitcher.

• Pour over ice cubes in tall glasses; garnish each with strawberry or lime wedge, if desired.   *Makes 6 servings*

Thai Coconut Iced Tea

Strawberry Lemonade

2 cups DOLE® Frozen Sliced or Whole Strawberries, partially thawed

3 cups cold water, divided

½ cup fresh lemon juice

½ cup sugar

Ice cubes

Fresh mint sprigs (optional)

PLACE strawberries in blender or food processor container with 1 cup water. Cover; blend until smooth. Add remaining 2 cups water; blend until smooth.

POUR mixture through strainer into large pitcher. Stir in lemon juice and sugar; add more sugar if necessary to taste.

POUR into ice-filled glasses; garnish with mint sprigs, if desired.

Makes 5 servings

Prep Time: 15 minutes

Vanilla Soda

1½ teaspoons sugar or equivalent artificial sweetener

1 teaspoon WATKINS® Vanilla

1 cup club soda

1 scoop vanilla ice cream

Combine sugar and vanilla in bottom of tall glass; mix well. Pour in club soda, stirring gently to blend. Carefully add ice cream to glass; serve with straw and long spoon.

Makes 1 serving

Strawberry Lemonade

Atsalot O' Apricot

1 (15-ounce) can of apricot halves, drained, juice reserved
1 cup crushed ice
½ cup chopped dried apricots, plus additional for garnish
¼ cup apricot preserves
    Fresh sage (optional)

1. Combine canned apricots, apricot juice, ice, ½ cup dried apricots and preserves in blender; blend until smooth.

2. Pour into two chilled glasses. Garnish with additional dried apricots and sage. Serve immediately.   *Makes 2 servings*

CARNATION® Green Tea Cooler

4 cups boiling water
6 green tea bags
1 tablespoon honey or more to taste
1 cup *dry* NESTLÉ® CARNATION® Instant Nonfat Dry Milk
    Ice cubes
4 fresh lime wedges

POUR boiling water over tea bags in glass or ceramic pitcher. Let steep for 10 minutes; remove tea bags. Stir in honey. Cool and refrigerate for at least 2 hours. Stir in dry milk.

TO SERVE: pour cooler over ice in glasses. Serve with lime wedges. Coolers can be sweetened with additional honey.   *Makes 4 servings*

Prep Time: 15 minutes
Cooling Time: 2 hours refrigerating

Atsalot O' Apricot

Lemon-Lime Icee

4 cups ice cubes, plus additional if necessary

2 cans frozen limeade concentrate

1 cup sparkling water

Juice of 1 lemon

Lemon and lime slices (optional)

1. Crush 4 cups ice in blender. Add frozen juice concentrate, sparkling water and lemon juice; blend until smooth. Add additional ice cubes to blender if thicker consistency is desired.

2. Pour into two glasses. Garnish with lemon and lime slices. Serve immediately. *Makes 2 servings*

Easy Orange Fizz

Maraschino cherries

Mint leaves

1 (6-ounce) can frozen Florida orange juice concentrate, thawed

Club soda or tonic water, chilled

Thoroughly drain maraschino cherries. Arrange mint leaves and cherries in compartments of ice cube trays; fill with water and freeze until firm to form decorative ice cubes.

Prepare orange juice concentrate according to label directions, except substitute club soda or tonic water for the water. Pour into glasses over decorative ice cubes. Serve at once. *Makes 4 servings*

*Favorite recipe from **Florida Department of Citrus***

Lemon-Lime Icee

Frozen Watermelon Whip

1¾ cups ice cubes
1 cup coarsely chopped seedless watermelon
1 cup brewed lemon herbal tea, at room temperature
Lime slices (optional)

1. Combine ice, watermelon and tea in blender; blend until smooth.

2. Pour into two tall glasses. Garnish with lime slices. Serve immediately.

Makes 2 servings

Nectarine Punch Cooler

1 pint fresh strawberries
2 medium fresh California nectarines, halved, pitted and cut into wedges
1 can (6 ounces) frozen pineapple or cranberry juice concentrate
12 ice cubes, cracked
1 to 2 cups sparkling water
Additional nectarine wedges for garnish

Hull strawberries. Reserve 6 whole strawberries for garnish. Add remaining strawberries, nectarines and frozen juice concentrate to blender. Process until smooth. Add ice and process until smooth. Pour into punch bowl or large container. Stir in sparkling water. Ladle into glasses. Serve with reserved strawberries and some additional nectarine wedges threaded onto stirrers.

Makes 6 servings

*Favorite recipe from **California Tree Fruit Agreement***

Frozen Watermelon Whip

Cherry Lemon Cooler

3 cups water

1 cup sugar

1 cup Northwest fresh sweet cherries, halved and pitted

Crushed ice

1 cup fresh lemon juice, refrigerated

1 bottle (1 liter) club soda or seltzer

Northwest fresh sweet cherries with stems

4 long stems fresh mint

Combine water and sugar in small saucepan; add halved cherries. Bring mixture to boil; reduce heat and simmer 5 minutes. Remove from heat and cool to room temperature. Strain syrup into container with tight fitting lid; discard cherries. Refrigerate syrup until cold. Fill a tall 12- to 16-ounce glass with ice. Pour ¼ cup lemon juice and ⅓ cup syrup over ice and top with club soda. Garnish with cherries and mint.

Makes 4 servings

Tip: Leftover syrup may be stored, refrigerated, up to one week.

*Favorite recipe from **Northwest Cherry Growers***

Honey Lemonade

Concentrate

> 6 tablespoons honey
>
> 1 cup lemon juice
>
> 1 lemon, thinly sliced

Mixer

> Ice cubes
>
> 1 quart carbonated water

For concentrate, dissolve honey in lemon juice in 1-quart jar or glass bowl. Add lemon slices and refrigerate until ready to use.

For mixer, fill 12-ounce glass with ice cubes. Add ¼ cup lemon juice concentrate and fill glass with carbonated water.   *Makes 4 servings*

Tip: Garnish with a lemon wedge.

*Favorite recipe from **National Honey Board***

Ginger-Cucumber Limeade

1½ cups chopped, seeded and peeled cucumber

⅓ cup frozen limeade concentrate, thawed

1 teaspoon grated fresh ginger

1 cup club soda or sparkling water, chilled

Ice cubes

Thick cucumber slices

Lime peel (optional)

1. Combine chopped cucumber, concentrate and ginger in blender; blend until nearly smooth. Combine cucumber mixture and club soda in 1-quart pitcher; gently stir.

2. Pour over ice and cucumber slices into three glasses. Garnish with lime peel. Serve immediately. *Makes 3 servings*

Orange Mist

6 cups V8® 100% Vegetable Juice

1 can (6 ounces) frozen orange juice concentrate, thawed

1½ cups seltzer water or orange-flavored seltzer water

Ice cubes

Stir the vegetable juice and orange juice concentrate in a large pitcher. Add the seltzer water. Serve over ice. *Makes 10 servings*

Prep Time: 5 minutes
Total Time: 5 minutes

Ginger-Cucumber Limeade

Lemon-Lime Watermelon Agua Fresca

10 cups seedless watermelon cubes

1 cup ice water

⅓ cup sugar

2 tablespoons fresh lemon juice

2 tablespoons fresh lime juice

Ice cubes

1. Combine half of watermelon and water in blender; blend until smooth. Transfer to bowl. Repeat with remaining watermelon and water. Stir in sugar, lemon and lime juices; mix until dissolved. Refrigerate until ready to serve.

2. Pour over ice into six glasses. Serve immediately.   *Makes 6 servings*

Red Grape Cooler

1 cup red grapes

2 cups club soda

1 tablespoon sugar

Combine all ingredients in blender or food processor. Blend thoroughly. Strain. Serve over ice.   *Makes 2 servings*

Variation: For a bubbly drink, blend only 1 cup club soda with grapes and sugar. Strain. Add remaining cup club soda to strained liquid.

*Favorite recipe from **The Sugar Association, Inc.***

Lemon-Lime Watermelon Agua Fresca

Berry Frost

1½ cups ice cubes

1 cup brewed raspberry herbal tea, room temperature

1 cup water

½ cup frozen unsweetened blueberries

1 tablespoon lime juice

½ teaspoon lime peel

1. Combine ice, tea, water, blueberries, lime juice and peel in blender; blend until smooth.

2. Pour into two tall glasses. Serve immediately. *Makes 2 servings*

Cherry Fizz

1 cup 100% ready-to-drink tart cherry juice

2 cups frozen unsweetened tart cherries

1 (6-ounce) can frozen pink or regular lemonade concentrate, undiluted

6 to 8 ice cubes

1 (12-ounce) can lemon-lime carbonated beverage, chilled

Orange and lime slices, for garnish

Put cherry juice blend and frozen cherries in an electric blender container; purée until smooth. Add lemonade concentrate and ice cubes; blend until smooth. Pour mixture into a 2-quart pitcher. Stir in lemon-lime carbonated beverage. Garnish with orange and lime slices. Serve immediately. *Makes 6 servings*

*Favorite recipe from **Cherry Marketing Institute***

Berry Frost

Lemon and Pomegranate Refresher

⅓ cup plus 1 tablespoon sugar, divided

   Ice cubes

4 lemon slices

3 bags hibiscus-lemon tea

1½ cups boiling water

1½ cups pomegranate juice

3 tablespoons fresh lemon juice

1 cup club soda, well chilled

   Lemon peel (optional)

1. Wet rims of four glasses with water, then dip into 1 tablespoon sugar. Fill with ice and lemon slices.

2. Place tea bags in large heatproof pitcher. Add boiling water. Steep tea 5 minutes. Remove and discard tea bags. Refrigerate until cold.

3. Combine tea, pomegranate juice, remaining ⅓ cup sugar and lemon juice in tall pitcher. Stir well. (This can be done in advance and kept chilled for several hours.) Just before serving, pour in the club soda and stir to mix.

4. Pour into prepared glasses. Garnish with lemon peel. Serve immediately.

Makes 4 servings

Lemon and Pomegranate Refresher

Orange Tea Zinger

2 orange or tangerine herbal tea bags

1 cup boiling water

   Ice cubes

2 cans (12 ounces) unsweetened seltzer water

   Orange wedges (optional)

1. Steep tea bags in boiling water 4 minutes. Remove tea bags and refrigerate until cool.

2. Pour half of cooled tea (just less than ½ cup) over ice into each of two tall glasses. Fill glasses with seltzer water and stir gently. Garnish with orange wedges. Serve immediately.   *Makes 2 servings*

Fresh Fruit Lemonade

1 to 1½ cups sliced ripe strawberries, whole raspberries or blueberries
   Juice of 6 SUNKIST® lemons (1 cup)

1 cup sugar

4 cups cold water

1 fresh SUNKIST® lemon, unpeeled, cut into cartwheel slices
   Ice cubes

In blender or food processor, combine berries, lemon juice and sugar; blend until smooth. Pour into large pitcher. Add cold water, lemon cartwheel slices and ice; stir well. Garnish each serving with additional fruit and/or fresh mint leaves, if desired.   *Makes about 6 servings*

Orange Tea Zingers

Honeydew Agua Fresca

¼ large honeydew melon, cut into small chunks and chilled
¼ cup fresh lime juice
¼ cup fresh mint leaves, plus additional for garnish
2 tablespoons sugar
1½ cups club soda, chilled
4 to 5 lime wedges (optional)

1. Combine melon, lime juice, ¼ cup mint and sugar in blender; blend until smooth. (Mixture may be blended in advance and chilled for several hours.)

2. Pour mixture into 4-cup measuring cup and stir in enough club soda to measure 4 cups.

3. Pour into four glasses. Garnish with lime wedges and additional mint. Serve immediately.

Makes 4 servings

Most melons are available fresh all year long. But the peak season for honeydew is June through October.

Honeydew Agua Fresca

Acknowledgments

The publisher would like to thank the companies and organizations listed below for the use of their recipes and photographs in this publication.

ACH Food Companies, Inc.

California Tree Fruit Agreement

Campbell Soup Company

Cherry Marketing Institute

Chilean Fresh Fruit Association

Cream of Wheat® Cereal

Crystal Farms®

Dole Food Company, Inc.

Equal® sweetener

Florida Department of Citrus

Michigan Apple Committee

National Cherry Growers & Industries Foundation

National Honey Board

National Watermelon Promotion Board

Nestlé USA

North Carolina SweetPotato Commission

Northwest Cherry Growers

Peanut Advisory Board

Polaner®, A Division of B&G Foods, Inc.

Stonyfield Farm®

The Sugar Association, Inc.

Reprinted with permission of Sunkist Growers, Inc. All Rights Reserved.

Unilever

U.S. Highbush Blueberry Council

Washington State Fruit Commission

Watkins Incorporated

Index

A

Anti-Stress Smoothie, 48
Apple
  Apple Smoothie, 14
  Cinnamon-Apple Smoothie, 68
  Mixed Berry Smoothie, 56
  Vermont Maple Smoothie, 30
Apple Smoothie, 14
Apricot
  Atsalot O' Apricot, 164
  Strawberry Mango Smoothie, 50
Atsalot O' Apricot, 164

B

Banana
  Anti-Stress Smoothie, 48
  Banana Blast Smoothie, 76
  Banana-Coconut "Cream Pie" Smoothie,
    124
  Banana-Pineapple Breakfast Shake, 24
  Banana Pudding Smoothie, 130
  Banana Smoothie, 10
  Banana Split Smoothie, 108
  Berry-Banana Breakfast Smoothie, 12
  Blackberry-Peach-Banana Smoothie, 93
  Blueberry Banana Oatmeal Smoothie, 16
  Breakfast Pom Smoothie, 28
  Cherry Smoothie, 26
  Chocolate Banana Peanut Butter
    Smoothie, 74
  Cinnamon-Apple Smoothie, 68
  Cool & Creamy Fruit Smoothies, 88
  DOLE® Sunrise Smoothie, 28
  Dreamy Banana Shakes, 154
  Energy Smoothie, 8
  Fruity Green Tea Smoothie, 38
  Fruity Smoothie, 96
  Honey Bear Smoothie, 62
  Honeydew Ginger Smoothie, 88
  "Hot" Chocolate Smoothie, 114
  Island Delight Smoothie, 42
  Morning Glory Cream Fizz, 18
  Peachy Banana Smoothie, 60
  Peanut Butter Banana Blend, 82
  Piña Colada Smoothie, 120
  Pineapple Berry Smoothie, 50
  Pineberry Smoothie, 106
  Pour-It-On Peanut Butter Smoothie, 72
  Power Punch Smoothie, 60
  Soy Milk Smoothie, 106
  Spiced Maple, Banana & Oatmeal
    Smoothie, 20
  Spiced Passion Fruit-Yogurt Smoothie, 104
  Strawberry Banana Coconut Smoothie,
    58

Banana (continued)
  Strawberry Sundae Smoothie, 126
  Tropical Sunrise, 32
  Wake-Me-Up Breakfast Smoothie, 18
  Wow Watermelon Smoothie, 80
Banana Blast Smoothie, 76
Banana-Coconut "Cream Pie" Smoothie,
    124
Banana-Pineapple Breakfast Shake, 24
Banana Pudding Smoothie, 130
Banana Smoothie, 10
Banana Split Smoothie, 108
Beat-the-Heat Tea Shake, 140
Berry-Banana Breakfast Smoothie, 12
Berry Berry Mango Smoothie, 110
Berry Blue Smoothie, 70
Berry Frost, 176
Berry Morning Medley, 22
Blackberry: Blackberry-Peach-Banana
    Smoothie, 93
Blackberry-Peach-Banana Smoothie, 93
Black Forest Smoothie, 121
Blueberry
  Anti-Stress Smoothie, 48
  Berry Blue Smoothie, 70
  Berry Frost, 176
  Blueberry Banana Oatmeal Smoothie, 16
  Blueberry Cherry "Cheesecake" Smoothie,
    121
  Blueberry Pineapple Smoothie, 38
  Blueberry Pomegranate Fruit Smoothie,
    24
  Blueberry Pomegranate Smoothie with
    Honey & Orange, 34
  Fruity Smoothie, 96
  Mixed Berry Smoothie, 56
  Purplicious Pomegranate Smoothie, 82
Blueberry Banana Oatmeal Smoothie, 16
Blueberry Cherry "Cheesecake" Smoothie,
    121
Blueberry Pineapple Smoothie, 38
Blueberry Pomegranate Fruit Smoothie, 24
Blueberry Pomegranate Smoothie with Honey
    & Orange, 34
Breakfast Mocha Java, 26
Breakfast Pom Smoothie, 28

C

Cantaloupe
  Cantaloupe Strawberry Shake, 144
  Nectarine Cantaloupe Smoothie, 44
Caramel: Mint-Caramel Tornado, 132
CARNATION® Green Tea Cooler, 164
Carrot Cake Smoothie, 112
Chai Soy Protein Smoothie, 12

Index

Cherry
Black Forest Smoothie, 121
Blueberry Cherry "Cheesecake" Smoothie, 121
Cherry-Berry Smoothie, 64
Cherry Cooler, 70
Cherry Fizz, 176
Cherry Lemon Cooler, 170
Cherry Smoothie, 26
Cherry Vanilla Chilla, 74
Easy Orange Fizz, 166
Maraschino Cherry Shake, 141
Red Velvet Shake, 136
Cherry-Berry Smoothie, 64
Cherry Cooler, 70
Cherry Fizz, 176
Cherry Lemon Cooler, 170
Cherry Smoothie, 26
Cherry Vanilla Chilla, 74
Chocolate
Banana Split Smoothie, 108
Black Forest Smoothie, 121
Breakfast Mocha Java, 26
Chocolate Banana Peanut Butter Smoothie, 74
Chocolate Chocolate Cookie Shake, 146
Christmas in July, 148
Cocoa-Nut Shake, 152
Frozen Hot Chocolate, 156
"Hot" Chocolate Smoothie, 114
Irish Cream Iced Cappuccino, 14
Mint-Caramel Tornado, 132
Mint Chocolate Chip Milkshakes, 152
Peanut Butter Chocolate Twist Shake, 148
Raspberry Chocolate Smoothie, 62
Raspberry Cocoa Freeze, 78
Razzmatazz Shake, 75
Red Velvet Shake, 136
S'mores Amore Smoothie, 128
Tiramisu Smoothie, 118
TOLL HOUSE® Chocolate Chip Cookie Milkshake, 138
Chocolate Banana Peanut Butter Smoothie, 74
Chocolate Chocolate Cookie Shake, 146
Christmas in July, 148
Cinnamon-Apple Smoothie, 68
Cocoa-Nut Shake, 152
Coconut
Banana-Coconut "Cream Pie" Smoothie, 124
Cocoa-Nut Shake, 152
Kiwi Chai Smoothie, 56
Kiwi Pineapple Cream, 56
Nuts for Coconuts, 64
Peanut Butter Chocolate Twist Shake, 148

Coconut *(continued)*
Piña Colada Milkshake, 142
Piña Colada Smoothie, 120
Piña Colada Smoothie Base, 120
Strawberry Banana Coconut Smoothie, 58
Thai Coconut Iced Tea, 160
Tropical Breeze Smoothie, 47
Tropical Mango Strawberry Protein Smoothie, 52
Tropical Sunrise, 32
Coffee
Breakfast Mocha Java, 26
Frosty Five-Spice Coffee Shake, 150
Irish Cream Iced Cappuccino, 14
Tiramisu Smoothie, 118
Cookies & Graham Crackers
Chocolate Chocolate Cookie Shake, 146
Pumpkin Pie Milkshake, 144
S'mores Amore Smoothie, 128
TOLL HOUSE® Chocolate Chip Cookie Milkshake, 138
Cool & Creamy Fruit Smoothies, 88
Cranberry
Cherry-Berry Smoothie, 64
Cranberry Orange Smoothie, 44
Cranberry Pineapple Smoothie, 46
Cranberry Pineapple Smoothie Base, 46
Cranberry Orange Smoothie, 44
Cranberry Pineapple Smoothie, 46
Cranberry Pineapple Smoothie Base, 46
Creamy Pineapple Shake, 138
Cucumber: Ginger-Cucumber Limeade, 172

D
Dates: Dessert Date Smoothie, 122
Dessert Date Smoothie, 122
DOLE® Sunrise Smoothie, 28
Dreamsicle Smoothie, 122
Dreamy Banana Shakes, 154

E
Easy Orange Fizz, 166
Emerald City, 66
Energy Smoothie, 8

F
Fresh Fruit Lemonade, 180
Frosty Five-Spice Coffee Shake, 150
Frozen Hot Chocolate, 156
Frozen Watermelon Whip, 168
Frozen Yogurt & Ice Cream
Anti-Stress Smoothie, 48
Beat-the-Heat Tea Shake, 140
Carrot Cake Smoothie, 112
Chocolate Chocolate Cookie Shake, 146

Index

Frozen Yogurt & Ice Cream (*continued*)
  Christmas in July, 148
  Cocoa-Nut Shake, 152
  Creamy Pineapple Shake, 138
  Dessert Date Smoothie, 122
  Dreamy Banana Shakes, 154
  Frosty Five-Spice Coffee Shake, 150
  Frozen Hot Chocolate, 156
  Green Tea Smoothie, 92
  Horchata Shake, 134
  "Hot" Chocolate Smoothie, 114
  Iced Tea Float, 140
  Irresistible Peach Smoothies, 126
  Mango Milk Shakes, 150
  Maraschino Cherry Shake, 141
  Mint Chocolate Chip Milkshakes, 152
  Mint-Caramel Tornado, 132
  Peanut Butter Chocolate Twist Shake, 148
  Piña Colada Milkshake, 142
  Pour-It-On Peanut Butter Smoothie, 72
  Pumpkin Pie Milkshake, 144
  Pumpkin Spice Smoothie, 76
  Purple Cow Jumped Over the Moon, 75
  Purple Power Shake, 142
  Raspberry Cocoa Freeze, 78
  Razzmatazz Shake, 75
  Red Tea Harvest Strawberry Smoothie, 102
  Root Beer Barrel Shake, 154
  S'mores Amore Smoothie, 128
  Strawberry Frozen Yogurt Smoothie, 114
  Sunshine Shake, 142
  Tiramisu Smoothie, 118
  TOLL HOUSE® Chocolate Chip Cookie Milkshake, 138
  Vanilla Soda, 162
Fruity Green Tea Smoothie, 38
Fruity Smoothie, 96

G
Gelatin Fruit Smoothie, 72
Ginger-Cucumber Limeade, 172
Glorious Morning Smoothie, 16
Going Green, 52
Grape
  Going Green, 52
  Grape Roughie, 36
  Purple Cow Jumped Over the Moon, 75
  Purple Power Shake, 142
  Red Grape Cooler, 174
Grape Roughie, 36
Grapefruit: Space Coast Smoothie, 80
Green Tea Smoothie, 92
Guava Smoothie, 22

H
Honey Bear Smoothie, 62
Honeydew
  Going Green, 52
  Honeydew Agua Fresca, 182
  Honeydew Ginger Smoothie, 88
  Lemon Melon Crème Smoothie, 130
Honeydew Agua Fresca, 182
Honeydew Ginger Smoothie, 88
Honey Lemonade, 171
Horchata Shake, 134
"Hot" Chocolate Smoothie, 114

I
Iced Tea Float, 140
Irish Cream Iced Cappuccino, 14
Irresistible Peach Smoothies, 126
Island Delight Smoothie, 42

J
Jump Start Smoothie, 10

K
Key Lime Pie Refresher, 132
Kiwi
  Going Green, 52
  Kiwi Chai Smoothie, 56
  Kiwi Pineapple Cream, 56
  Soy Strawberry Kiwi Smoothie, 90
  Strawberry Kiwi Smoothie, 90
  Watermelon Kiwi Smoothie, 40
Kiwi Chai Smoothie, 56
Kiwi Pineapple Cream, 56

L
Lemon
  Cherry Fizz, 176
  Cherry Lemon Cooler, 170
  Fresh Fruit Lemonade, 180
  Frozen Watermelon Whip, 168
  Honey Lemonade, 171
  Irresistible Peach Smoothies, 126
  Lemon and Pomegranate Refresher, 178
  Lemon Chiffon Cooler, 116
  Lemon-Lime Icee, 166
  Lemon-Lime Watermelon Agua Fresca, 174
  Lemon Mango Smoothie, 78
  Lemon Melon Crème Smoothie, 130
  Light Lemon Strawberry Smoothie, 84
  Raspberry-Lemon Smoothie, 47
  Sparkling Pomegranate Gingerade, 158
  Strawberry Lemonade, 162
  Watermelon Yogurt Mint Smoothie, 110

Index

Lemon and Pomegranate Refresher, 178
Lemon Chiffon Cooler, 116
Lemon-Lime Icee, 166
Lemon-Lime Watermelon Agua Fresca, 174
Lemon Mango Smoothie, 78
Lemon Melon Crème Smoothie, 130
Light Lemon Strawberry Smoothie, 84
Lime
    Berry Frost, 176
    Emerald City, 66
    Ginger-Cucumber Limeade, 172
    Honeydew Agua Fresca, 182
    Key Lime Pie Refresher, 132
    Kiwi Chai Smoothie, 56
    Kiwi Pineapple Cream, 56
    Lemon Mango Smoothie, 78
    Lemon-Lime Icee, 166
    Lemon-Lime Watermelon Agua Fresca, 174
    Piña Colada Smoothie, 120
    Piña Colada Smoothie Base, 120
    Strawberry Limeade, 160

M
Mandarin Orange Smoothie, 94
Mango
    Berry Berry Mango Smoothie, 110
    Island Delight Smoothie, 42
    Jump Start Smoothie, 10
    Lemon Mango Smoothie, 78
    Mango-Ginger Smoothie, 36
    Mango Milk Shakes, 150
    Mango Smoothie, 100
    Mangorange Madness, 54
    Strawberry Mango Smoothie, 50
    Tropical Breeze Smoothie, 47
    Tropical Mango Strawberry Protein Smoothie, 52
    Tropical Sunrise, 32
Mango-Ginger Smoothie, 36
Mango Milk Shakes, 150
Mango Smoothie, 100
Mangorange Madness, 54
Maple
    Spiced Maple, Banana & Oatmeal Smoothie, 20
    Vermont Maple Smoothie, 30
Maraschino Cherry Shake, 141
Marshmallows: S'mores Amore Smoothie, 128
Mint
    Cherry Lemon Cooler, 170
    Christmas in July, 148
    Easy Orange Fizz, 166
    Honeydew Agua Fresca, 182
    Mint-Caramel Tornado, 132

Mint *(continued)*
    Mint Chocolate Chip Milkshakes, 152
    Space Coast Smoothie, 80
    Watermelon Yogurt Mint Smoothie, 110
Mint-Caramel Tornado, 132
Mint Chocolate Chip Milkshakes, 152
Mixed Berries
    Berry Morning Medley, 22
    Breakfast Pom Smoothie, 28
    Fruity Smoothie, 96
Mixed Berry Smoothie, 56
Mixed Fruit: Yummy Fruit Smoothie, 66
Morning Glory Cream Fizz, 18

N
Nectarine Cantaloupe Smoothie, 44
Nectarine Punch Cooler, 168
Nuts for Coconuts, 64

O
Orange
    Blueberry Pomegranate Smoothie with Honey & Orange, 34
    Cherry Cooler, 70
    Cranberry Orange Smoothie, 44
    Dreamsicle Smoothie, 122
    Easy Orange Fizz, 166
    Glorious Morning Smoothie, 16
    Green Tea Smoothie, 92
    Iced Tea Float, 140
    Island Delight Smoothie, 42
    Mandarin Orange Smoothie, 94
    Mangorange Madness, 54
    Mango Smoothie, 100
    Orange Mist, 172
    Orange Tea Zinger, 180
    Peachy Banana Smoothie, 60
    Power Punch Smoothie, 60
    Rise 'n' Shine Smoothie, 32
    Sunshine Shake, 142
    Tropical Sunrise, 32
Orange Mist, 172
Orange Tea Zinger, 180
Over the Rainbow, 66

P
Papaya
    Morning Glory Cream Fizz, 18
    Papaya-Pineapple Smoothie, 54
Passion Fruit
    Red Tea Harvest Strawberry Smoothie, 102
    Spiced Passion Fruit-Yogurt Smoothie, 104
Peach
    Blackberry-Peach-Banana Smoothie, 93
    Cool & Creamy Fruit Smoothies, 88

Index

Peach (continued)
  Irresistible Peach Smoothies, 126
  Jump Start Smoothie, 10
  Mango-Ginger Smoothie, 36
  Mangorange Madness, 54
  Peachy Banana Smoothie, 60
  Peachy Keen Smoothie, 98
  Raspberry Peach Perfection Smoothie, 40
  Sunrise Smoothie, 30
Peachy Banana Smoothie, 60
Peachy Keen Smoothie, 98
Peanut Butter
  Chocolate Banana Peanut Butter
    Smoothie, 74
  Dreamy Banana Shakes, 154
  Peanut Butter Banana Blend, 82
  Peanut Butter Chocolate Twist Shake, 148
  Pour-It-On Peanut Butter Smoothie, 72
Peanut Butter Banana Blend, 82
Peanut Butter Chocolate Twist Shake, 148
Piña Colada Milkshake, 142
Piña Colada Smoothie, 120
Piña Colada Smoothie Base, 120
Pineapple
  Banana-Coconut "Cream Pie" Smoothie,
    124
  Banana-Pineapple Breakfast Shake, 24
  Berry Blue Smoothie, 70
  Blueberry Pineapple Smoothie, 38
  Cranberry Pineapple Smoothie, 46
  Cranberry Pineapple Smoothie Base, 46
  Creamy Pineapple Shake, 138
  DOLE® Sunrise Smoothie, 28
  Fruity Smoothie, 96
  Island Delight Smoothie, 42
  Kiwi Chai Smoothie, 56
  Kiwi Pineapple Cream, 56
  Nectarine Punch Cooler, 168
  Papaya-Pineapple Smoothie, 54
  Piña Colada Milkshake, 142
  Piña Colada Smoothie, 120
  Piña Colada Smoothie Base, 120
  Pineapple Berry Smoothie, 50
  Pineberry Smoothie, 106
  Sunrise Smoothie, 30
  Tropical Breeze Smoothie, 47
  Tropical Sunrise, 32
Pineapple Berry Smoothie, 50
Pineberry Smoothie, 106
Pomegranate
  Blueberry Pomegranate Fruit Smoothie, 24
  Blueberry Pomegranate Smoothie with
    Honey & Orange, 34
  Breakfast Pom Smoothie, 28
  Lemon and Pomegranate Refresher, 178

Pomegranate (continued)
  Purplicious Pomegranate Smoothie, 82
  Sparkling Pomegranate Gingerade, 158
Pour-It-On Peanut Butter Smoothie, 72
Power Punch Smoothie, 60
Pumpkin
  Pumpkin Pie Milkshake, 144
  Pumpkin Pie Smoothie, 103
  Pumpkin Spice Smoothie, 76
Purple Cow Jumped Over the Moon, 75
Purple Power Shake, 142
Purplicious Pomegranate Smoothie, 82

R
Raspberry
  Berry Berry Mango Smoothie, 110
  Berry Frost, 176
  Mixed Berry Smoothie, 56
  Purplicious Pomegranate Smoothie, 82
  Raspberry Chocolate Smoothie, 62
  Raspberry Cocoa Freeze, 78
  Raspberry-Lemon Smoothie, 47
  Raspberry Peach Perfection Smoothie, 40
  Raspberry Smoothie, 98
  Raspberry Soda Smoothie, 86
  Red Velvet Shake, 136
  Sunshine Shake, 142
Raspberry Chocolate Smoothie, 62
Raspberry Cocoa Freeze, 78
Raspberry-Lemon Smoothie, 47
Raspberry Peach Perfection Smoothie, 40
Raspberry Smoothie, 98
Raspberry Soda Smoothie, 86
Razzmatazz Shake, 75
Red Grape Cooler, 174
Red Tea Harvest Strawberry Smoothie, 102
Red Velvet Shake, 136
Rise 'n' Shine Smoothie, 32
Root Beer Barrel Shake, 154

S
S'mores Amore Smoothie, 128
Sherbet & Sorbet
  Cool & Creamy Fruit Smoothies, 88
  Emerald City, 66
  Lemon Chiffon Cooler, 116
  Lemon Mango Smoothie, 78
  Mandarin Orange Smoothie, 94
  Nuts for Coconuts, 64
  Over the Rainbow, 66
  Peachy Banana Smoothie, 60
  Piña Colada Milkshake, 142
  Purplicious Pomegranate Smoothie, 82
  Red Velvet Shake, 136
  Wow Watermelon Smoothie, 80

Index

Soda & Seltzer
Cherry Fizz, 176
Cherry Lemon Cooler, 170
Easy Orange Fizz, 166
Emerald City, 66
Ginger-Cucumber Limeade, 172
Honeydew Agua Fresca, 182
Honey Lemonade, 171
Lemon and Pomegranate Refresher, 178
Lemon-Lime Icee, 166
Morning Glory Cream Fizz, 18
Nectarine Punch Cooler, 168
Orange Mist, 172
Orange Tea Zinger, 180
Over the Rainbow, 66
Raspberry Soda Smoothie, 86
Razzmatazz Shake, 75
Red Grape Cooler, 174
Root Beer Barrel Shake, 154
Sparkling Pomegranate Gingerade, 158
Vanilla Soda, 162
Soy Milk Smoothie, 106
Soy Strawberry Kiwi Smoothie, 90
Space Coast Smoothie, 80
Sparkling Pomegranate Gingerade, 158
Spiced Maple, Banana & Oatmeal Smoothie, 20
Spiced Passion Fruit-Yogurt Smoothie, 104
Strawberry
Banana Split Smoothie, 108
Berry Berry Mango Smoothie, 110
Blueberry Pomegranate Fruit Smoothie, 24
Cantaloupe Strawberry Shake, 144
Cherry-Berry Smoothie, 64
Cool & Creamy Fruit Smoothies, 88
DOLE® Sunrise Smoothie, 28
Energy Smoothie, 8
Fresh Fruit Lemonade, 180
Gelatin Fruit Smoothie, 72
Glorious Morning Smoothie, 16
Island Delight Smoothie, 42
Jump Start Smoothie, 10
Light Lemon Strawberry Smoothie, 84
Mixed Berry Smoothie, 56
Nectarine Punch Cooler, 168
Pineapple Berry Smoothie, 50
Pineberry Smoothie, 106
Red Tea Harvest Strawberry Smoothie, 102
Rise 'n' Shine Smoothie, 32
Soy Milk Smoothie, 106
Soy Strawberry Kiwi Smoothie, 90
Spiced Passion Fruit-Yogurt Smoothie, 104
Strawberry Banana Coconut Smoothie, 58
Strawberry Frozen Yogurt Smoothie, 114
Strawberry Kiwi Smoothie, 90

Strawberry *(continued)*
Strawberry Lemonade, 162
Strawberry Limeade, 160
Strawberry Mango Smoothie, 50
Strawberry Sundae Smoothie, 126
Tropical Mango Strawberry Protein Smoothie, 52
Wake-Me-Up Breakfast Smoothie, 18
Wow Watermelon Smoothie, 80
Strawberry Banana Coconut Smoothie, 58
Strawberry Frozen Yogurt Smoothie, 114
Strawberry Kiwi Smoothie, 90
Strawberry Lemonade, 162
Strawberry Limeade, 160
Strawberry Mango Smoothie, 50
Strawberry Sundae Smoothie, 126
Sunrise Smoothie, 30
Sunshine Shake, 142
Sweet Potato: Power Punch Smoothie, 60

T
Tea
Beat-the-Heat Tea Shake, 140
Berry Frost, 176
Blueberry Pomegranate Fruit Smoothie, 24
CARNATION® Green Tea Cooler, 164
Frozen Watermelon Whip, 168
Fruity Green Tea Smoothie, 38
Green Tea Smoothie, 92
Iced Tea Float, 140
Lemon and Pomegranate Refresher, 178
Orange Tea Zinger, 180
Red Tea Harvest Strawberry Smoothie, 102
Strawberry Frozen Yogurt Smoothie, 114
Thai Coconut Iced Tea, 160
Thai Coconut Iced Tea, 160
Tiramisu Smoothie, 118
TOLL HOUSE® Chocolate Chip Cookie Milkshake, 138
Tropical Breeze Smoothie, 47
Tropical Mango Strawberry Protein Smoothie, 52
Tropical Sunrise, 32

V
Vanilla Soda, 162
Vermont Maple Smoothie, 30

W
Wake-Me-Up Breakfast Smoothie, 18
Watermelon
Frozen Watermelon Whip, 168
Lemon-Lime Watermelon Agua Fresca, 174

Index

Watermelon (*continued*)
  Watermelon Kiwi Smoothie, 40
  Watermelon Yogurt Mint Smoothie,
    110
  Wow Watermelon Smoothie, 80
Watermelon Kiwi Smoothie, 40
Watermelon Yogurt Mint Smoothie, 110
Wow Watermelon Smoothie, 80

Y
Yogurt (*see also* **Frozen Yogurt & Ice Cream**)
  Apple Smoothie, 14
  Banana Blast Smoothie, 76
  Banana-Pineapple Breakfast Shake,
    24
  Berry-Banana Breakfast Smoothie, 12
  Berry Berry Mango Smoothie, 110
  Berry Blue Smoothie, 70
  Berry Morning Medley, 22
  Black Forest Smoothie, 121
  Blackberry-Peach-Banana Smoothie,
    93
  Blueberry Banana Oatmeal Smoothie,
    16
  Blueberry Pomegranate Fruit Smoothie,
    24
  Chai Soy Protein Smoothie, 12
  Cherry Vanilla Chilla, 74
  Chocolate Banana Peanut Butter
    Smoothie, 74
  Cinnamon-Apple Smoothie, 68
  Cool & Creamy Fruit Smoothies, 88
  DOLE® Sunrise Smoothie, 28
  Dreamsicle Smoothie, 122
  Energy Smoothie, 8
  Fruity Smoothie, 96
  Glorious Morning Smoothie, 16
  Grape Roughie, 36
  Honeydew Ginger Smoothie, 88
  Island Delight Smoothie, 42
  Jump Start Smoothie, 10
  Kiwi Chai Smoothie, 56
  Kiwi Pineapple Cream, 56
  Lemon Melon Crème Smoothie, 130
  Light Lemon Strawberry Smoothie, 84
  Mandarin Orange Smoothie, 94
  Mango-Ginger Smoothie, 36
  Mangorange Madness, 54
  Mango Smoothie, 100
  Mixed Berry Smoothie, 56
  Morning Glory Cream Fizz, 18
  Nectarine Cantaloupe Smoothie, 44
  Peachy Keen Smoothie, 98
  Peanut Butter Banana Blend, 82
  Pineapple Berry Smoothie, 50

  Pineberry Smoothie, 106
  Power Punch Smoothie, 60
  Pumpkin Pie Smoothie, 103
  Raspberry Chocolate Smoothie, 62
  Raspberry-Lemon Smoothie, 47
  Raspberry Peach Perfection Smoothie,
    40
  Raspberry Smoothie, 98
  Raspberry Soda Smoothie, 86
  Razzmatazz Shake, 75
  Rise 'n' Shine Smoothie, 32
  Soy Strawberry Kiwi Smoothie, 90
  Space Coast Smoothie, 80
  Spiced Maple, Banana & Oatmeal
    Smoothie, 20
  Spiced Passion Fruit-Yogurt Smoothie,
    104
  Strawberry Kiwi Smoothie, 90
  Strawberry Sundae Smoothie, 126
  Sunrise Smoothie, 30
  Tropical Mango Strawberry Protein
    Smoothie, 52
  Tropical Sunrise, 32
  Vermont Maple Smoothie, 30
  Wake-Me-Up Breakfast Smoothie, 18
  Watermelon Kiwi Smoothie, 40
  Watermelon Yogurt Mint Smoothie, 110
Yummy Fruit Smoothie, 66

Metric Conversion Chart

VOLUME MEASUREMENTS (dry)

$^1/_8$ teaspoon = 0.5 mL
$^1/_4$ teaspoon = 1 mL
$^1/_2$ teaspoon = 2 mL
$^3/_4$ teaspoon = 4 mL
1 teaspoon = 5 mL
1 tablespoon = 15 mL
2 tablespoons = 30 mL
$^1/_4$ cup = 60 mL
$^1/_3$ cup = 75 mL
$^1/_2$ cup = 125 mL
$^2/_3$ cup = 150 mL
$^3/_4$ cup = 175 mL
1 cup = 250 mL
2 cups = 1 pint = 500 mL
3 cups = 750 mL
4 cups = 1 quart = 1 L

VOLUME MEASUREMENTS (fluid)

1 fluid ounce (2 tablespoons) = 30 mL
4 fluid ounces ($^1/_2$ cup) = 125 mL
8 fluid ounces (1 cup) = 250 mL
12 fluid ounces (1$^1/_2$ cups) = 375 mL
16 fluid ounces (2 cups) = 500 mL

WEIGHTS (mass)

$^1/_2$ ounce = 15 g
1 ounce = 30 g
3 ounces = 90 g
4 ounces = 120 g
8 ounces = 225 g
10 ounces = 285 g
12 ounces = 360 g
16 ounces = 1 pound = 450 g

DIMENSIONS

$^1/_{16}$ inch = 2 mm
$^1/_8$ inch = 3 mm
$^1/_4$ inch = 6 mm
$^1/_2$ inch = 1.5 cm
$^3/_4$ inch = 2 cm
1 inch = 2.5 cm

OVEN TEMPERATURES

250°F = 120°C
275°F = 140°C
300°F = 150°C
325°F = 160°C
350°F = 180°C
375°F = 190°C
400°F = 200°C
425°F = 220°C
450°F = 230°C

BAKING PAN SIZES

Utensil	Size in Inches/Quarts	Metric Volume	Size in Centimeters
Baking or Cake Pan (square or rectangular)	8 × 8 × 2	2 L	20 × 20 × 5
	9 × 9 × 2	2.5 L	23 × 23 × 5
	12 × 8 × 2	3 L	30 × 20 × 5
	13 × 9 × 2	3.5 L	33 × 23 × 5
Loaf Pan	8 × 4 × 3	1.5 L	20 × 10 × 7
	9 × 5 × 3	2 L	23 × 13 × 7
Round Layer Cake Pan	8 × 1½	1.2 L	20 × 4
	9 × 1½	1.5 L	23 × 4
Pie Plate	8 × 1¼	750 mL	20 × 3
	9 × 1¼	1 L	23 × 3
Baking Dish or Casserole	1 quart	1 L	—
	1½ quart	1.5 L	—
	2 quart	2 L	—